# The Church and Socialism in Cuba

# The Church and Socialism in Cuba

*Raúl Gómez Treto*

*Translated from the Spanish by*
*Phillip Berryman*

Maryknoll, New York 10545

The Catholic Foreign Mission Society of America (Maryknoll) recruits and trains people for overseas missionary service. Through Orbis Books, Maryknoll aims to foster the international dialogue that is essential to mission. The books published, however, reflect the opinions of their authors and are not meant to represent the official position of the society.

---

Originally published by Departamento Ecuménico de Investigaciones (San José, Costa Rica) as *La iglesia católica durante la construcción del socialismo en Cuba* © 1986 by Raúl Gómez Treto


Published by Orbis Books, Maryknoll, NY 10545
Manufactured in the United States of America


Manuscript editor: Lisa McGaw

---

ISBN 0-88344-574-3
ISBN 0-88344-573-5 (pbk.)

# Contents

# Foreword

*"The most beautiful gift that God has given me is my meeting with President Fidel Castro"*

—Mother Teresa of Calcutta,
Havana, July 1986

*"I must say that I've never heard anyone praise the Pope more highly than [President Castro]"*

—Cardinal John O'Connor of New York,
Havana, April 1988

These two quotations, taken from *Granma,* the newspaper that is the official organ of the Communist party of Cuba, give some indication of the astounding changes now taking place within the Cuban church. Although the actual number of practicing Catholics is quite small (between 100,000 and 200,000—or 1-2 percent of the population), changes in both the church itself and in church-state relations are proceeding at a pace and are of a magnitude that far outshadow these insignificant statistics. Put quite simply: after three decades of life within Latin America's first revolutionary political system, the church has finally come to terms with this reality, and has decided that its own position has to be *with* the people. In sum, it has matured after an extremely difficult period of confrontation with the government, dependence on external influence, and a lengthy period of soul-searching in the self-imposed catacombs of silence. It is this process that Raúl Gómez Treto, a leading Catholic lay leader throughout this time, documents in this concise and well-documented study.

This account by Gómez Treto is badly needed by all who are interested in the role and direction of the church. Overshadowed certainly by more dramatic events in Central America and the Southern Cone, the rapid development of liberation theology, the impact of Medellín and Puebla, the prophetic message of martyrs throughout Latin America, and a host of other factors, the Cuban church has been overlooked for too long. To a certain extent there was an understandable historical justification for this: the revolution (1959) had started before the sweeping winds of change emanating from Vatican II (1962–65) – much less Medellín (1968) – had carried to Cuba; for years before and after the revolution began, the church played a limited role in Cuba – a fact evidenced by the church's notorious lack of penetration in rural Cuba and the parallel dependence of the church on private schools for the middle-class in the cities; the church (composed mainly of Spanish clergy – trained, significantly, in Franco's Spain) was in essence the "church in Cuba" rather than the "Cuban church"; and, finally, many Catholic leaders directly opposed the revolutionary process. All these factors provided a poor foundation for any significant role to be undertaken by the church. Little wonder, then, that Nicaraguan Ernesto Cardenal would fulminate against the Cuban church some fifteen years ago, calling it – with some justification – the most reactionary in Latin America: there was simply little else to say about it.

Many significant changes have taken place in the last decade, however, and as a result Cuba has gradually rejoined the mainstream of Latin America. In tandem with this reincorporation of Cuba into the Latin American community has been the revival of the church itself – in no small measure after realizing that the continent's first socialist revolution was not about to collapse overnight. Many fascinating developments have taken place which have helped this process of revival – most of which are touched upon by Raúl Gómez Treto. Some of those developments include the maturation of a new generation of Cuban bishops and clergy; progressive pastoral messages and communiqués that have sought to make the church relevant to the contemporary world; a significant diplomatic effort by the

Vatican—and especially by nuncio Cesare Zacchi (in Cuba from 1962–1975)—to maintain open channels of dialogue; visits to Cuba by a variety of high profile church representatives (from Mother Teresa to the Rev. Jesse Jackson, Cardinal O'Connor to several Vatican and CELAM representatives); and the crucially important Encuentro Nacional Eclesial Cubano (National Convocation of the Cuban Church—ENEC), which took place in 1986. Also important in analyzing this equation are initiatives undertaken by the revolutionary government in general, and President Fidel Castro in particular: invitations to the more than one hundred clergy who attended a meeting on the international debt crisis in 1985; a flurry of meetings between the president and church leaders in the last four years (after a quarter-century of virtually no contact); the opening of the new Office of Religious Affairs attached to the secretariat of the party's Central Committee; extensive restoration work to dozens of older churches being undertaken largely at government expense; a clearly benign presentation of religious matters in the state-controlled media (after decades of hostility and criticism); a notable "watering-down" of party dogma concerning the church in all official documents; and finally the publication in 1985 by the Council of State of *Fidel y la Religión,* the long (379 pp.) interviews with Fidel Castro by Brazilian Dominican Frei Betto—a book which was an instant best-seller in Cuba, with more than a million copies sold. Clearly there are interesting developments afoot in both church and government circles.

Gómez Treto writes as a person who has witnessed first-hand all these changes, and who has much to say on them. Indeed as one of Cuba's leading lay leaders for many years he has participated actively—encouraging the church to "move with the times" and bear prophetic witness to these necessary changes. His is not the distant approach of a foreign academic, but rather is inextricably linked to the reality that he has lived—as a Catholic and (why not?) as a revolutionary, for three decades. Therein lies the book's strength.

Others would argue that his interpretations are incorrect, and that the church has not developed in the recent decade. Rather, they claim, the church has passed from a *modus vivendi* to a *modus moriendi,* having "sold out" to the revolutionary government in return for some short-lived material incentives and promises of future considerations. Certainly this would be the view of exiled Catholic lay leaders like Manuel Fernández and Pablo M. Alfonso.[1] Such a view is understandable—particularly since both writers have each been in exile for many years—but sadly is typical of the "pre-Vatican mindset" which has characterized the Cuban church for so long. The fact of thc matter is that the church in Cuba—albeit belatedly—*has* finally caught up with the mainstream of church social teaching. From being "foreigners in their own country" church representatives have finally found a niche for themselves in their *patria,* and have realized that their mission is to serve the people as a whole—not just the urban bourgeoisie. It is, then, the exiles who are sadly behind the times, dreaming of a triumphalist, hierarchical church of appearance rather than substance, sadly co-opted by the government of the day. They will never understand the reforms of John XXIII.

Having said that, Raúl Gómez Treto's last chapter ("Dialogue [1979–1985]) is perhaps a shade overly optimistic. Rather, one could argue that the period represents the solidification of a form of *modus vivendi,* with the actual "dialogue" just starting at the end of this period. This process has advanced successfully, and bears every indication that it will continue to do so in the post-1985 period. The church has given every indication that it is attuned to the reality of life in revolutionary Cuba ("Socialist society has helped us to give through justice what we previously gave out of charity," stated the 1986 Final Document of the ENEC), while Fidel Castro has gone out of his way to condemn any discrimination on the basis of religion, and to reiterate an invitation to John Paul II to visit Cuba. Meaningful dialogue, then, has indeed arrived.

It is important to bear in mind, however, that this is not just a book about the Cuban church during the construction of a socialist process. On the contrary, the experience of the Cuban church during this period could prove an invaluable lesson for the church in other areas of Latin America where a desire to turn back the hands of time to pre-Vatican II days is still found. One can learn from a study of the Cuban case history how easily the church can lose touch with changing political reality and, fearful of losing its earthly benefits, cling to traditionally held privileges. Similarly, the idea that the church shouldn't "get involved in politics" is laid to rest: *everything* the church does is "political"; it is simply a matter of how best to exercise that influence in the light of the gospel, and not self-interest. Much can also be gleaned concerning the idea of religious divisions and a "parallel church," since as the Cuban case shows clearly, if the church is to be true to its mandate, it has to adhere to its preferential option for the poor—and not alienate itself from the masses. Church leaders throughout Latin America can also learn not to fear the very concept of revolution or to provide a bulwark behind which the contras of their day could scheme to destroy the revolutionary process: as the Cuban experience shows, those types of attitudes and actions greatly damage church credibility among the people as a whole. Furthermore, the church has to be with the people in their struggle for a better life, and if the people support the revolutionary goals (whether the hierarchy or priests and religious like them or not), the church needs to accompany them if it is to have any relevance at all in the new society. These are all difficult lessons, and have yet to be learned by many church leaders—particularly in Central America. Perhaps all of these suggestions are best summed up in the words of Msgr. Adolfo Rodríguez, President of the Cuban Episcopal Conference, in his opening address to the ENEC in February 1986 in Havana. In that address Msgr. Rodríguez explained the kind of church that he and the others present hoped to see flourish in Cuba:

> A church that wishes to be a sign of communion, to be a part of the people, since otherwise it would indeed be an "opium of the masses," and would cease to be the church. . . . The Cuban church has to be the church of openness and dialogue, with our hands extended, and our doors open.[2]

JOHN KIRK
May 1988

# The Church and Socialism in Cuba

# Introduction

This short history of the Catholic church in Cuba since 1959 was prepared at the behest of the Commission for Research into Latin American Church History (CEHILA) and forms part of a vast project of writing the full history of the church in Latin America. The present work is the result of an effort carried out with the help of associates who have provided extremely valuable information and judgments. Others have been writing the history of Protestant churches in Cuba in a parallel effort. Some day both works will have to be combined so as to present a history of the (Christian) church in Cuba, but the time is not ripe for such an effort at integration.

This work has been carried out under severe constraints. Other responsibilities, both secular and religious, have left me very little time for historical research. The need to be brief also makes this effort correspondingly more difficult.

The history of the Catholic church in Cuba falls into three parts, following a natural division of Cuban history into three periods: the colonial, republican-bourgeois, and socialist. This volume concerns the history of the socialist period; it covers the time from the revolutionary victory (1959) until shortly before the writing of this book. Works by CEHILA on the colonial and republican-bourgeois periods are currently underway, and although this book is intended to stand on its own, in time it will be essential to view the content of the present book in relation to the works being written about the other periods.

In writing this work, I have had to contend with enormous

problems. No one in Catholic circles wanted to take responsibility for seeing it through, although other people would have had more time than I. Moreover, I am not a historian, do not claim to be one, and am not going to become one; I am simply a personal witness to a series of events experienced within my church. Due to a personal motivation growing out of my faith, I recognized that, despite my shortcomings, I had to undertake this modest contribution. Others more capable than I will be able to take it up and expand and develop it further, in a more scholarly and definitive way.

In order to help explain this work I feel I should make certain observations. In history we must distinguish between history as it is made and as it is written. The history of the church is the community life of Christians throughout time and within the social context in which the church has unfolded, both locally and overall. Written history, or historiography, has history as its object. Nevertheless, historiography is also history. Historians also make history insofar as they do not simply present the picture of a dead past, but are also themselves carrying out an activity that is as political as the activity of the people in the events they present.

When one seeks to narrate the unfolding of history, one inevitably analyzes, interprets, and projects it in a way that is colored by one's own personality, itself formed in and connected with the social, economic, and political context in which one lives, develops, and takes leisure. Like all human beings, historians are political beings who have made more or less conscious political choices in a society that is politically organized in some fashion. Historians may have much or little awareness of the political nature of their actions, including that of writing history. If they are unaware, they run the risk of being manipulated (in the worst sense) by others, either directly or through ideological mediations that are not their own; thus they may see their own intentions frustrated when they discover (to their horror) that the effects have been different from, or even the opposite of, what they intended. Today honest historians cannot ignore the political nature of their work; to claim to be apolitical is the highest degree of dishonesty. Any effort aimed at recounting history (like any effort to make history) must be conscious of its political function and hence must take on the intentionality appropriate to the historian's ideological position.

Writing history is thus a way of making history. Historians must ask: Who is writing? What are they writing about? For whom are they writing? The historian's work entails complete tactics and strategy (the short- and long-range aim), which is political in nature.

With regard to church history, it is undeniable that from the outset the church has always played a political role in all the societies in which it has existed and carried out its activity. Although its role should always have been prophetic, the church has often been tolerant of social sin and even in complicity with it. Simply reading most ecclesiastical histories (and antiecclesiastical ones as well) is enough to show how this political role of the church has been whisked away, intentionally hidden by both apologists and opponents.

A project like CEHILA's effort to write the full history of the church in Latin America is no doubt something new, since the aim is not to write a church history in the traditional apologetic mode or in the critical mode of the various sorts of atheists and anticlericalists. CEHILA is striving to write a history of the church with a critical thrust and following scholarly norms, while all the while having its viewpoint grounded in the reality of the people of Latin America. Rather than being the object of missions, these people have suffered invasion and colonization with Christian banners flying in front. No doubt the apologists and those who benefit from ecclesial status will find the reorganization of the information and the new version thereby produced more or less harsh, but those on the antiecclesiastical side may find that it is incorrect or does not go far enough.

To undertake the history of the church in Cuba within the CEHILA project naturally has features of its own. I do not find it chauvinistic to think that we Cubans who have experienced the revolutionary social, economic, and political process that has been taking place in our country for more than twenty-five years probably have a greater responsibility when it comes time to analyze the activity of our church. In this connection, with all due respect, I believe that the lay experience has been different from that of the clergy. When I say "lay," I mean those lay Christians who are fully a part of the social structures of our country. Unfortunately, the clergy of our country have not been able to become a part of those structures, nor have those "faithful" who follow them.

Another element I take into consideration is of a more theological nature. Most ecclesiastical histories consider the church to be hierarchical structures, for those structures have taken on the role of representing the church, and within it they hold sway over the rest of the believers, whom they have in mind when they refer to the "faithful."

In my church, the Catholic church, the notion of the church-as-community was relegated to a subordinate position and the prevailing idea was that of the church-as-hierarchy. In this study I take as my starting point the idea of the church-as-community, more or less structured or organized for good or for ill. I understand the ecclesial community as a part of a wider community, namely, the society within which the church develops and functions. This idea was taken up once more by Vatican Council II, even though in many aspects, places, and levels it is not really put into practice. The acceptance of the church as being "part of the people"—at least in theory—is beginning to become common throughout Latin America, including Cuba, more recently—due to the irrepressible force of Christian base communities and the liberation theology they have developed.

One particular feature of Cuban religiosity is the fact that the original indigenous culture has had almost no influence on Cuban culture due to its primitive nature and because it was rapidly wiped out by colonialism. The reverse is true of the African culture that came over with the slaves and which, upon being integrated into the Hispanic culture of the colonizers, gave birth to an Afro-Cuban culture that has had a decisive influence on Cuban popular religiosity. As a consequence of both roots, popular religiosity is less Christian in nature, appearances to the contrary notwithstanding.

As to my sources of information, unfortunately the revolutionary period (1959 onward) in the history of the Cuban church is not very well documented, and existing documentation is not only hard to locate but also rather inaccessible to an ordinary researcher. Hence, to a great extent I have made use of my own intense experiences of the Catholic church in Cuba during these years of the revolutionary period and the access that that experience has afforded to what was really happening within the church. Thus it is my intention to provide initial firsthand information, albeit concise and indeed largely testimonial in nature. Further, as regards methodological and formal aspects of this work, let me indicate the following points.

1. Although I try to give as much information as possible, for reasons of space and time I have had to withhold, for a subsequent and more ambitious effort, many details that would no doubt clarify the present text.

2. I decided to use quasi-narrative or chronicle style so as to be as informative as possible about a period for which there is not a great deal of objective information—or worse, about which there is a great deal of disinformation. Moreover, such a style makes the text more accessible to a wider circle of readers.

3. Out of respect for the reader I have refrained from offering many personal judgments about the events presented. In an initial presentation it seemed more respectful to provide the facts and allow readers to judge for themselves about the existence, life, mission, and relations of the church during this intense period of Cuban history.

4. At the end of this book, in the chapter titled "Conclusions," I have made an attempt at a brief analysis of the signs that a new period in the life of the church is underway.

In reference to the overall structure of the present work, I have grouped the main developments in the Cuban church since 1959 into five phases, preceded by an overview of the general situation of the church.

The first phase, "Uneasiness," covers parts of 1959 and 1960, namely, the brief democratic-popular time of an agrarian and anti-imperialist nature, which initiated the transition from capitalism to socialism in Cuba. There are some who have sought to present church-state relations during this phase as being that of a "honeymoon," an "agreement"—in which the church supported the revolution. However, through my own experience I know that during this period the hierarchical and clerical leadership of the church tried to influence the direction of the revolution so as to prevent it from being radicalized or turning toward communism. When that effort failed, the church felt uneasy.

The second phase, "Confrontation," began in 1960 and lasted until 1963. This was the stage at which a good portion of the hierarchy and clergy together with the better-off among the faithful, finding itself unable to control the revolution, decided to combat it head-on in alliance with, or as an instrument of, the other reactionary forces in Cuba and outside it. There was an effort to manipulate popular religious feeling in order to pit believers against the revolution. This political effort on the part of the church hierarchy and the clergy was unsuccessful. Many believers left the church and opted for the revolution, and thus began the process by which the church absented itself from the social and political realm, and large numbers of believers left the church. Finally, without spilling any blood, the so-called "expulsion of priests" from the country completely undid the counterrevolutionary network that made use of a part of the clergy.

The third phase, "Flight," saw the hierarchical and clerical leadership of the church focused on encouraging many Catholic families or individuals to flee the country. This effort furthered the emigration of technical and professional people as well as those from the sectors most under the influence of the clergy and of counterrevolutionary propaganda. This new development also contributed to emptying the churches in the country, due to the emigration of the most devoted churchgoers. This characterized the situation until around 1967.

The fourth phase, "Re-encounter," was marked by the influence of the Second General Conference of Latin American Bishops held in Medellín, Colombia, in 1968. Two pastoral letters of the Catholic bishops stand out during this phase, one condemning the imperialist blockade of Cuba, and the other urging that Catholics on the island be involved in labor concerns. Both letters helped reverse the situation begun with the anticommunist and counterrevolutionary pastoral letters prepared during the first phase. This attitude did not mean support for the revolution, but it did begin a stage of overcoming the contradictions between church and state.

The work done during this phase in Cuba's revolution extends approximately to the year 1979, that is, the time of the third CELAM conference, at Puebla, Mexico, which marked the starting point for a new phase, whose signs are quite contradictory. The church had become mature enough to begin a prophetic dialogue process with the revolutionary accomplishments among the people, but there were still many reasons to fear a reversal.

In this fifth and most recent phase, "Dialogue," the hopeful expectations of the previous phase have been fulfilled. After the "re-encounter" of the previous phase there occurred a real and effective institutional exchange of opinions and suggestions between the official representatives of the churches and those of the state and the party. The Third Congress of the Cuban Communist party (PCC); the National Convocation of the Cuban Church (ENEC),[1] a Catholic convocation; and, on the Protestant side, the annual assembly of the Ecumenical Council of Cuba (CEC), and of other Christian churches and ecumenical movements, closed the phase—or perhaps better, opened a new era in which the dialogue that is in fact underway shows promise of becoming institutionalized in order to serve a collaboration that will be mutually critical and dialectically profitable for all the Cuban people. It may well serve as an example for others.[2]

# 1

# The General Situation of the Church before 1959

On January 1, 1959, as the people's revolutionary movement under the leadership of Fidel Castro overthrew the tyranny of Fulgencio Batista, there began a new period in the Cuban political process, with all its economic and social consequences. There also began a new period in the role played by the Catholic church in the history of the Cuban people, of which it has long been a part, although its influence has varied and indeed has been contradictory.

The revolutionary changes that began to take place in Cuba caught the church by surprise, since historically and theologically it was still "preconciliar." Twenty-five days later Vatican Council II was to be announced by Pope John XXIII, but sessions would not begin until 1962 and it was not to conclude until 1965. The church universal was guided by the Thomism that had been made official in the sixteenth century by the Council of Trent. Fully in communion with Rome but quite dependent on the conservative Spanish church, the Cuban church contributed nothing to enrich those traditionalist frameworks. Even during the 1950s any evolutionary notion of creation was banned from Catholic classrooms, pulpits, catechism classes, and confessionals; the hierarchical idea of the church completely overshadowed its community dimension; and the church's mission was conceived and carried out as wholesale but sporadic sacramentalizing in rural areas far from urban and suburban churches and parishes.

Although most of the bishops were Cuban, they were decisively influenced by the fact that the bulk of the clergy, both diocesan and religious, was Spanish, as were most sisters. The patriotic figures of Father Varela and other outstanding Cuban clergy from previous centuries were not highly regarded in ecclesiastical circles. They were mentioned in Catholic schools only because of the requirements of the state history and literature curriculum imposed by the Ministry of Education.

In this context, the most progressive elements were some lay movements or groups whose positions on social questions went no further than a reformism, more or less under the inspiration of the neo-Thomism of Jacques Maritain, Leon Bloy, and others. Most of the Catholic leaders who in some manner or other took a stand against the Batista tyranny came from these groups. Their aspirations were of an ethical nature and were limited to the establishment of a representative democracy that could put into effect a kind of social justice, consisting of employee stockholding and profit sharing and of a general moral clean-up by means of an all-out assault on drug addiction, gambling, prostitution, and misuse of public funds.

## Organizational Structure

At the beginning of 1959 the church was organized into two archdioceses and four dioceses, along the lines of the six provinces into which Cuba was then divided. Archbishop Enrique Pérez Serantes presided over the see of Santiago de Cuba, whose dioceses were those of Camagüey and Cienfuegos, headed by Bishops Riú Anglés and Eduardo Martínez Dalmau. His Eminence Cardinal Manuel Arteaga y Betancourt headed the archdiocese of Havana. His auxiliary was Bishop Alfredo Müller Sanmartín, and the dioceses were Pinar del Río and Matanzas, headed by Bishops Evelio Díaz Cía and Alberto Martín Villaverde. The Cuban Bishops Conference, which at that time had been only recently created, was still practically in an experimental stage and amounted to no more than occasional meetings of the bishops in order to exchange impressions.

According to the report given by the Cuban bishops at CELAM's First General Conference (Río de Janeiro, 1955) there were 220 diocesan priests, who were mainly Spanish; only 95 were Cuban. There were three minor seminaries, located in Havana, Santiago de Cuba, and Matanzas, with some 114 seminarians; and a single major seminary in Havana with 19 seminarians.

There were some 461 priests in male religious orders,[1] of whom only 30 were Cuban. Adding these to the diocesan priests gave a total of some 681 priests in what was then a country of slightly less than six million inhabitants. There were also some 329 members of these orders who were not ordained to the priesthood, most of them also foreign. The female orders included some 1,872 sisters, of whom only 556 were Cuban; 1,167 were involved in teaching. The Jesuits, Salesians, and Franciscans had novitiates, with a total of 146 students at various stages, and the Christian Brothers and Marists had novitiates to prepare religious for teaching, with a total of 17 students.

Large numbers of practicing Catholics were members of hundreds of religious societies—those of the Blessed Sacrament, the Virgin of Loreto, of Fatima, of the Holy Rosary, of Our Lady of Charity, and so forth. In addition, there were the Franciscan, Dominican, Carmelite, and Servite[2] third orders; the Apostolate of Prayer, the Marian Congregations (Daughters of Mary, Catholic University Association, and so forth), the Knights of Columbus, the Daughters of Isabel, the Legion of Christ, the Legion of Mary, the St. Vincent de Paul Society, the Movement of Catholic Professional People and Intellectuals, the Catholic Doctors, Catholic Artists, and so forth, as well as Italian-style Catholic Action, with its four branches and its specialized youth movements. The Cursillos de Cristiandad were just beginning to be organized.

All these religious confraternities, congregations, and associations had their own funding deriving from membership dues; only occasionally did they receive any additional economic help from the hierarchy, the clergy, or religious orders.

Theoretically these organizations of the Catholic laity—with priests providing leadership if not presiding directly—were more or less effective auxiliary forms of the hierarchical apostolate. During that period there began an effort to bring them into the notion of the hierarchical apostolate carried out by Catholic Action, although this effort produced misunderstanding, opposition, and problems.

Given the prevailing ecclesiology, however, in practice these organizations, rather than being genuine agencies for evangelizing society, were in fact the church's secular forces, ecclesiastical society's way of being present within society at large. Through their "Catholic influence" they enabled the church to remain stable and make progress.

Moreover, the church's faithful consisted of those who went to church regularly, as well as those who went occasionally and who called themselves "Catholics." This mass of believers, more or less Catholic or syncretist and coming from all levels of society, was said to amount to over 90 percent of the Cuban population. The assumption, deceptive but widespread in Latin America, was that all those who had been baptized as children should be considered Catholic, even if they did not fulfill the other ecclesiastical rites or precepts, did not live the gospel consistently, and had no adequate doctrinal formation.

According to the only statistical study from this period, carried out and published by the Catholic University Association of Havana in 1956, in a population of some six million inhabitants about 72.5 percent claimed to be Catholic, 19 percent indifferent, 6 percent Protestant, 1 percent spiritist, 0.5 percent Masonic, 0.5 percent Jewish, and 0.5 percent devoted to saints. Of the 72.5 percent who were "Catholics," 75 percent said they were not practicing Catholics, and of the remaining 25 percent, only 11 percent said they received the sacraments regularly (which amounts to 2 percent of the population of the country).[3]

## Apostolic Works

In those days the church viewed its apostolate as proselytizing and saw its aim as restoring a new Christendom both throughout the continent and locally, along the lines of the model of European Christendom, which was itself already dead. Utilizing the prevailing social theology to bypass the contradictions of the existing capitalist system and keeping moral theology confined to interpersonal relations, the church carried out its apostolate through its numerous works of mercy, which took institutional form in schools, clinics, orphanages, old people's homes, cemeteries, and so forth. The original prophetic sign of such institutions was overshadowed by the fact that they provided social services subsidiary to those of the state, alongside of, and in competition with other such institutions whether religious or lay.

In 1955 there were 212 Catholic schools (belonging to both religious orders and parishes), which were educating some 61,960 students (in a potential school population of around two million children and young people ranging from seven to eighteen years of age; thus students in Catholic schools made up no more than 2.5 percent of the school-age population of the country at that time). The male proportion of those attending Catholic schools was only 30 percent. There were three Catholic universities, one of them Jesuit, a more recent one set up by the Christian Brothers, and St. Thomas of Villanova University, which belonged to Augustinian priests from the United States, and which had an enrollment of only 1,000, generally from the most well-off sectors of the capital city.[4]

The church owned and took care of twenty children's homes, twenty-one old people's homes, three hospitals for adults and two for children, a psychiatric sanatorium, a leper colony, an orphanage, a women's clinic, and a number of other clinics and places in which one could have free doctor's visits.[5]

These ecclesiastical works by no means satisfied the needs of the people. Their relatively limited scope and the fact that they were concentrated in cities, and indeed in well-off neighborhoods—the only way they could make ends meet and perhaps turn a profit—meant that most people did not benefit from them. This situation was not a scandal in a dependent, consumption-minded, underdeveloped capitalist society where the overriding principle was that of profit. On the contrary, the limited extent of these works carried out by the church for the poor of the nation was in itself a prophetic sign of what a society more just than the existing one would be, but the sign was insufficient and scarcely noticeable.

The church's apostolate was also carried out in catechetical activity and in pious works that took institutional form in countless religious societies and in apostolic associations and congregations.

Subsequently, when the socialist state took over providing the social services of teaching, public health, and so forth and extended them to the whole population, the church no longer provided these services as extensively as before. By 1970 the church owned and administered only three old people's homes, a hospital, a psychiatric hospital, a home for handicapped children, and a home for old women. This was all that remained of its former works besides the services provided by some sisters in state-care centers. This new situation was painfully obvious in the church's pastoral uneasiness during those years. The fact that the church still had catechetical centers in church communities, parishes, and family settings, and the freedom to engage in liturgy and worship within the local churches was not enough to give direction to a renewed overall pastoral approach in a new society.

## Economic and Social Relationships

The material situation in which the church found itself at the end of the *Patronato Real* (detailed regulations over the colonies) imposed by the Spanish Crown was overcome by means of the economic negotiations for reparation that were formalized under United States intervention and military rule and later by means of unofficial relationships with successive elected governments, despite the official separation of church and state. In reality, the Catholic church enjoyed preferential treatment over other religious bodies in the country, and that gave it unique social, economic, and even political weight.

The Cuban bishops' report to CELAM's First Conference, held in Río de Janeiro (1955), stated that

> despite the prevailing laicism, the church and the state have maintained very good relations in Cuba. Indeed, the state

> gives special treatment to the church, since Catholicism is the religion of the majority of the Cuban people and it provides economic assistance for building churches and schools and for the church's charitable works, although this aid is not given on a regular basis and does not appear in the national budget.[6]

Even though the ecclesiastical territories in Cuba were considered mission territory, the church, and especially religious orders, sent large sums of money to their mother houses in Spain and Rome. All this furthered the prevailing notion that Cuba was "Catholic" when the revolutionary process got underway.

Compared to churches in other Latin American and European countries, the Cuban church did not invest well. It was not a large absentee landowner like some of the other churches in Latin America. Its main investments in real estate were urban and its financial activity was concentrated in mortgage loans on urban properties. Its greatest source of income was parishes, many of which were in the hands of religious orders, and Catholic schools. Other activities were kept more or less at the break-even point. There was no accounting or budget control over the ecclesiastical economy as a whole, and the result was a doubly contradictory relationship; on the one hand, the church was seemingly independent, yet in reality it was dependent on the popular sectors that made up much of the faithful and likewise on the economically privileged in the country, who kept it going financially and whose interests were in contradiction to those of the popular class. The church was lax about religious syncretism, on one side, and loose morals, on the other.

The church's relationships with other religious and social sectors in the country and the mindset it had toward them are reflected in the 1955 report to the Río de Janeiro Conference already mentioned.

> Protestantism is unquestionably making a great effort to conquer more ground among the Cuban people, who are Catholic by tradition. . . . Thus Protestantism is a serious danger, which must be thwarted.

> The predominant kind of spiritism is not the scientific kind, but rather, a Catholicism that is watered down with various superstitious practices. . . . This superstitution is present especially among colored people, peasants, and the most uncultivated poor classes of the population. It is a result of religious ignorance.
>
> In Cuba, Freemasonry is organized similarly to the way it is elsewhere. It has lodges set up in almost every town in the country. . . . In Cuba, Masonry does not have the spirit of aggressive hostility against the Catholic church that it has in other countries, especially in Europe. . . . However, some are really sectarian and hostile to the church, especially in the higher reaches of Masonry. In general, it can be said that although Masonry does not fight the church directly in Cuba, it nevertheless does great damage because it keeps thousands of men away from the church; although they may claim otherwise, one may not be a Catholic and a Mason at the same time. In addition, Freemasonry strives to preserve the errors of religious indifference as well as the lay character of the state and of education.
>
> At present, communism is illegal in Cuba and the authorities pursue those who spread it. . . . Although the Cuban working class is not in agreement with communist ideas, it feels gratitude toward some of its leaders, who struggle for the economic and social betterment of that class.[7]

## Relations of the Holy See with the Cuban Government

Such relationships, which had existed during the Spanish imperial government, were established with the republican government of Cuba in 1935 and they have continued up to the present. On January 1, 1959, Bishop Luis Centoz was the apostolic nuncio. Although he had maintained official and even personal relations with the tyrant Batista, he helped some Catholics who one way or another were involved in the struggle against the tyranny to escape the regime's repression. His successors were

Bishops Cesare Zacchi, Mario Tagliaferri, Giuseppe Laigueglia, and Giulio Einaudi.

The Cuban government's representative to the Vatican had ambassadorial status in 1959. Contrary to the case of other Latin American countries, Cuba and the Apostolic See never signed any concordat. Dr. Luis Amado Blanco, a Catholic, was the revolutionary government's ambassador to the Holy See from the beginning of the revolution until his death in Rome in 1975. He had carried out that function for fourteen years, and toward the end of his life he was also the dean of the diplomatic corps in the Roman see. He was succeeded by Dr. J. Portuondo and then by Dr. Estévez.[8]

## The Church during the Socialist Revolution

Since the revolutionary victory on January 1, 1959, and the subsequent social changes, the church has been involved in a new situation, one for which it was not prepared.

Institutionally the church did not take part in the popular liberation struggles against the tyranny just as it did not take part in the emancipation struggles of the nineteenth century. The revolutionary activity of those Catholics who took part in the insurrection stage, symbolized by Father Guillermo Sardiñas, who held the rank of *comandante* in the Rebel Army, and the student martyr, José Antonio Echeverría, seem to have been motivated more by patriotism than by faith. Father Camilo Torres had not yet given his Christian witness of "effective love" in Colombia.

As a matter of fact, the ecclesiastical institution seemed quite at home in the dependent capitalist society of the bourgeoisie of the republic, then almost six decades old. Many distinguished Catholics, both clerical and lay, proved to have had too many connections with the overthrown regime. Moreover the upper and middle classes could not even conceive of the possibility of a structural change in the country. The only thing most Catholics wanted was that the moral life of their country be cleaned up. As a whole, the church was not striving for radical changes, nor did it believe a socialist revolution was feasible; indeed, in such a revolution it would have seen a threat to its own future activity.

Thus the church was caught by surprise by a society it had believed was docile and faithful to it, and which soon began to move and change quickly and radically without it. The revolution was going to be carried out with the church, without the church, or even against the church. From its inception almost five centuries before, the Cuban church had never taken the initiative in the history of the country, and now it could only react to the developments taking place around it. The way it reacted at this socialist moment in Cuban history can be summarized schematically in five phases. Although it is not easy to specify the time limits, these phases can be characterized in the following manner: (1) uneasiness, 1959–60; (2) confrontation, 1961–62; (3) flight, 1963–67; (4) re-encounter, 1968–78; (5) dialogue, 1979–85.

# 2

# Uneasiness (1959–1960)

For several reasons the church hierarchy was led to hope that Cuba's newly victorious revolution would not affect the church institutionally: the fact that notable ecclesiastics like Archbishop Enrique Pérez Serantes had supported revolutionary leaders during the insurrection; the fact that priests like Father Guillermo Sardiñas, a *comandante* in the Rebel Army, and other Catholics had taken part in the struggle; the fact, moreover, that some bishops (such as Bishop Eduardo Martínez Dalmau), who could have led to restrictions being put on the church, left the country immediately; and finally the fact that some leaders from the Catholic laity were in important administrative positions in the revolutionary government. Prompted by this hope, some Catholic groups even sought to have religious teaching introduced into public schools.

Nevertheless, the church's defensive attitude, consonant with the official theology of that period, at the same time induced in the hierarchy, the clergy, and the better-off sectors of the faithful a feeling of fear and mistrust toward the phenomenon of revolution—a phenomenon they found disconcerting—which boldly stated that it acknowledged no commitment to those sectors that had traditionally been dominant in the country. Fear of laicism, naturalism, socialism, and communism, which existing papal doctrine condemned so harshly, produced a deep-seated mistrust of the revolution in the leading sectors of the Cuban church, although it was not manifested publicly.

This situation of uneasiness led the hierarchy to act with the utmost prudence initially, so as to avoid tensions that could deprive the church of influence over events or push the revolutionary government too far in a radical direction. The church's ideological stance prevented the hierarchy from realizing that the limited nature of the reforms it could accept would inevitably stand in contradiction to a deep-seated revolutionary process such as the one beginning in Cuba. The triumphalist and absolutizing ecclesiology of Christendom, then ascendant, placed the church in the middle of the path along which the people in revolution were advancing. Collision would be inevitable.

## Important Changes in the Catholic Hierarchy

At the moment when the Batista tyranny was overthrown through armed struggle, the Catholic church in Cuba had a cardinal, Archbishop Manuel Arteaga Betancourt of Havana, a man of old Cuban stock from Camagüey, whose career had been quite controversial. Among his good qualities, however, was the fact that he had stayed out of the struggle for ecclesiastical power, when, around 1924, while he was still a young priest, there was a crisis, and Archbishop Pedro González Estrada of Havana resigned. He had also stood out for his efforts to "Cubanize" the Catholic clergy in the country, by always supporting native priestly vocations and supporting the promotion of Cuban priests to the episcopacy.

At that time the island was divided into six dioceses. The archdiocese of Santiago de Cuba was headed by the beloved Archbishop Enrique Pérez Serantes who, although he had been born in Tuy, Galicia, in Spain, had deep understanding for the Cuban people, from the time he was made bishop of Camagüey before accepting the see of Santiago. He played an outstanding role in connection with Fidel Castro's 1953 failed attack on the Moncada barracks when he appealed to the dictatorial authorities not to kill him—as they often did with their political enemies—but to put him on trial in the normal manner according to the law. The dioceses were those of Camagüey, headed by Bishop Carlos Riu Anglés, who was also Spanish-born, and Cienfuegos, under Bishop Eduardo Martínez Dalmau.

The Havana archdiocese's suffragan sees were Pinar del Río, headed by Bishop Evelio Díaz Cía, and Matanzas, led by Bishop Alberto Martín Villaverde, both of whom were Cuban. Bishop Alfredo Müller Sanmartín served as auxiliary to the archbishop of Havana.

Shortly after the demise of the dictatorship, Bishop Martínez Dalmau of Cienfuegos left the country and resigned from the episcopacy. The reasons for his decision were never revealed. There were rumors that it was his own and his family's economic ties to figures in the toppled regime that prompted the decision. That was surprising given the fact that during the 1940s the bishop had carried on a public dispute with the editors of the ultraconservative *Diario de la Marina,* in defense of Cuban cultural values. Bishop Alfredo Müller took over the see of Cienfuegos, no longer serving as auxiliary in Havana.

Given the transfer of Bishop Müller and the advanced age of Cardinal Arteaga, Bishop Evelio Díaz of Pinar del Río was appointed auxiliary bishop of Havana and titular bishop of Landia (April 24, 1959), and Bishop Manuel Rodríguez Rozas was made a bishop in order to serve the diocese of Pinar del Río. On November 14, 1959, Bishop Evelio Díaz was made titular archbishop of Petra di Palestina and coadjutor archbishop of Havana, with right of succession, and thus he administered the archdiocese until the cardinal's death in 1963.

In view of the complexity of the see of Havana, which was also the capital of the country, two auxiliary bishops were appointed, Bishop José Maximino Domínguez and Bishop Eduardo Boza Masvidal, both of them Cubans who were ordained bishops for that purpose. Shortly afterward, however, in 1960, Bishop Domínguez was transferred to provide pastoral leadership in the dioceses of Matanzas after the death of Bishop Martín Villaverde, and the revolutionary government expelled Bishop Boza from the country in 1961, accusing him of involvement in counterrevolutionary activity. The archdiocese had no auxiliaries until 1964, when, with Bishop Evelio now fully in office, Bishop Alfredo Llaguno y Canals and Bishop Fernando Azcárate Freyre de Andrade were made his auxiliaries.

## Church Reaction to the Initial Revolutionary Measures

The measures of the revolution described here, like those that followed, were intended to benefit the broadest popular sectors. That meant of necessity that the interests of privileged sectors would be affected. To the extent the church, as an institution or some sectors of it, shared in those privileges, they would be affected by the revolutionary legislation. Such cases included the canceling of university degrees, the lowering of rents, and the agrarian and urban reforms.

The law enacted January 11, 1959, declared null all degrees granted by private and state universities after November 30, 1956, except those granted by the universities of Havana, Las Villas, and Santiago de Cuba. That was the date of the uprising of the population of Santiago de Cuba, which paved the way for the landing of Fidel Castro a few days later. At that time the University Student Federation (FEU) called for a student strike in support of those revolutionary actions, but only the students at the state universities observed it. That is why they were exempted from the effects of the law. The idea was that those affected by the measure had taken advantage of their own failure to support the insurrectionary struggle. The measure was directly harmful to the three Catholic universities and to other religious universities as well as those that had been granted permission to function by the administration of the tyrant Batista. The Catholic hierarchy made no public protest over this measure, which affected only those sectors of Catholicism that were socially and economically most privileged. All it did was to make some fruitless efforts to soften their impact.

The March 1959 law cutting rents in half for all urban renters in the country directly affected the small landlord sector in Cuban society, which sought to avoid the uncertainty of other investments by putting its money into urban real estate. The church and its orders, congregations, and associations felt the impact of this measure economically, but it did not make any public protest, since the law obviously benefited the people.

The constitutional law of agrarian reform, decreed on May 17, 1959, had a greater impact on the economic power structure of the landholding class, both Cuban and transnational. As church, Cuban Catholicism was not very much affected by this measure, since the institutional church did not have large landholdings in Cuba. Despite the fact that Catholic landholders were affected and even invoked moral theology and papal teaching to question the forms of compensation set up by the law, demonstrations in support of the agrarian reform were held in a number of churches. Indeed collections were taken up in order to donate agricultural equipment to the beneficiaries of the law, and they were channeled through the National Agrarian Reform Institute.

In the midst of these contradictions that were taking place within the church, the newspaper *Diario de la Marina* on its own sought to declare itself the spokesperson of Cuban Catholicism in order to criticize systematically the popular measures taken by the revolution. This newspaper, which had begun in 1832 as a mere record of transactions in the port of Havana, for several generations had represented the economic interests of the most conservative and tradition-bound dominant sectors in the country. At the close of the nineteenth century, during the wars for emancipation, it had rejoiced when the Deputy General of Independence, Antonio Maceo, fell in battle, and in the twentieth century it supported the falangist government in Spain. It had recently reinforced its self-appointed role as Catholic spokesperson by making the archbishop of Havana, Cardinal Manuel Arteaga y Betancourt, the symbolic president of its advisory board. Some of the bishops, who were among the most conservative in the whole Latin American continent, considered it "the best newspaper in the world."[1] Ultimately it was nationalized along with the rest of the privately owned press.

## Father Biaín and the Magazine *La Quincena*

Quite different from the stance of *Diario de la Marina* was that of *La Quincena*. In their own printshop the Franciscans put out a traditional kind of magazine called *San Antonio*. During the 1950s this publication broadened its perspective, first under the name *Semanario Católico* and later as a magazine with a modern and social outlook called *La Quincena,* which may be regarded as the most important Catholic publication in Cuba. It became, as its masthead indicated, "A Christian response to the problems of today." The distinguished intellectual, Father Angel Gaztelu, worked on the magazine. This magazine's prestige was due to a Basque-born Franciscan friar, Father Ignacio Biaín.

Father Biaín, a widely acknowledged intellectual, drew to the magazine a group of young people who exemplified the most up-to-date thought among Catholics at that time, and he reprinted from foreign sources many articles exemplifying the most advanced Catholic social thought. In his editorials he interpreted the revolution positively and with a view toward the future. Under pressure from his superiors, he turned over the magazine to a new staff at the end of 1959, but *La Quincena* did not survive the change and ceased to appear in early 1960, by decision of its editors.

Biaín had been in contact with underground forces fighting the Batista tyranny, and he had provided encouragement for many Catholic young people in their insurrectionary yearnings. Open to any kind of ideological advance, he sought to make it clear that the Cuban Revolution was the great historic moment of the liberation of Cuba. This attitude rubbed some people the wrong way in the Catholic church and even in his own order. Father Biaín died in Havana on November 15, 1963, surrounded by his Franciscan order. His funeral rites were celebrated in the Church of San Francisco in the capital, from which the funeral procession set out to the Cristóbal Colón Cemetery, where his remains lie.

## The National Catholic Congress

The first occasion on which the church confronted the revolution institutionally was the organization and celebration of the National Catholic Congress in November 1959. The congress was preceded by the National Assembly of Cuban Catholic

Action, including all four of its branches. At this meeting the leadership was completely changed.

The congress was celebrated in the Plaza of the Revolution dedicated to José Martí, in front of the statue of that apostle of Cuba's independence. From the eastern town of El Cobre the revered image of the Virgin Mary of La Caridad was brought in a procession the length of the island. The finale of the congress was the November 29 torchlight procession, which wound its way in the rain through the city of Havana, and brought together in the plaza tens of thousands of the faithful from all levels of society.

Presiding over the congress from the platform and altar were all the bishops of Cuba, along with other prelates and religious superiors and the new leadership of the Cuban laity. On the right was the special place for the state authorities as well as for the clergy, the religious communities, the diplomatic corps, and the national and foreign press. Representing the revolutionary government at the major ceremony was Dr. Osvaldo Dorticós Torrado, president of the republic, and Dr. Fidel Castro Ruz, prime minister of the government at that point, as well as other leading figures of the revolution, such as *Comandante* Juan Almeida.[2]

At that moment, the official position of the Cuban Catholic church became clearly defined. José Ignacio Lazaga, a lay leader, expressed it as follows:

> . . . The old idea dividing any enterprise into two parts, capitalists on the one hand and proletarians on the other, like two adversarial forces condemned to perpetual struggle, should be replaced by a new conception that would enable all who participate in an enterprise, whether as capitalists or workers, to feel equally owners and co-sharers in the effort and in the profits. . . . Communism, and in general any kind of totalitarian socialist regime, dispossesses all, since there is only one owner, the State. . . . Catholic thought is opposed to communist and Marxist teachings, and generally to all teachings that propose that the human being be subordinated to the totalitarian State.[3]

A woman leader, Clara Lucas Azcona, stated:

> Class prejudices must be erased by means of a like-minded determination to triumph that can unite hearts in the pursuit of an ideal. We must take up the same problems together, be aware of the same weaknesses, so as to be aware that no obstacle is a match for the sum total of energy that comes from unselfish collaboration. . . . Those of us here are black, mulatto, white, yellow, . . . and when we pray we all say, "Our Father." . . . Can there be, then, any separation of races . . . ? Are there differences of social class . . . ? Is there a discrimination between the privileged and the forgotten . . . ? *No!*[4]

A different and more serious approach, but one that unfortunately was less heeded at that time, was presented by Mateo Jover, a youth leader.

> Human beings are social beings. Their natural state is life in relationship with others. They have been created by God to live in society, and only in that fashion are they complemented and do they perfect their individual personality. They contribute to society and receive from it. They must offer their best efforts so that later they may receive in hundredfold the benefits that the social body provides for them. . . . If this is true for all human beings it is supremely so for Christians. [He quoted His Holiness, Pius XII:] "In this [social] realm . . . only one attitude is forbidden: withdrawal. That would not be emigration but desertion." . . . Those who call themselves Catholic and do not carry out their duties toward their country are not only bad citizens, but bad Christians.

Finally, Jover provided a basis for international solidarity when he said:

> Moreover, we have the right, as does any country, to prefer certain nations. Those that are connected to us through cultural similarity, those who share common interests with

> us, those who have aided us, those who are in worst shape and most oppressed, have special claims on our love and our preaching.[5]

In his closing words at the congress, Bishop Alberto Martín Villaverde of Matanzas said, "This congress, which should have been called the Catholic Congress to Defend Our Lady of Charity, was necessary, because today as never before, there is an effort to root out of people the very idea of God; but without God, the very reason for true love among human beings vanishes."[6] Archbishop Enrique Pérez Serantes of Santiago de Cuba wrote of the congress:

> This magnificent Catholic Congress, which we have just celebrated, has proclaimed to the whole world two facts, among others. First, that the Cuban people are Catholic . . . and should be understood as Catholic; since they have been Catholic from the beginning, it is a despicable error to put Catholicism on the same level as the rest of the foreign and tiny denominations, and even worse on the level of nonreligious or irreligious bodies. Second, that the bond that most unites Cubans, making them forget anything that might divide them, is devotion to the Blessed Virgin, under the title of *La Caridad del Cobre,* which is Cuban to the core.[7]

There was a striking difference in focus between laity and bishops.

In the *Boletín de las Provincias Eclesiásticas de Cuba,* the official publication of the dioceses of Cuba (year 43, nos. 1–2, January–February 1960), in which the foregoing statements were published, there was also the statement made by CELAM at the end of its meeting held in Fomeque, Colombia, November 8–15, 1959. The section headings of that statement were "Deceits of Communism," "Incompatibility of Communism and Christianity," and "The True Face of Communism." CELAM's influence was not helpful to the church in Cuba.

The social sectors affected by the revolutionary measures taken saw the National Catholic Congress as the chance to mobilize the population, made up primarily of believers, so as to put a brake on the direction they feared the revolution was taking. For their part, the mass of believers saw in the congress a way to show publicly their gratitude to Our Lady of Charity for the people's victory over tyranny and injustice and to harmonize their faith with their vigorous patriotism. The positions were quite at odds, but the church was not alert enough to grasp how deeply opposed the positions were. The revolutionary tremors shaking society after a long period of lethargy and despair began to make clear the class contradictions operating in society and in the church itself, for the church is part of society. These contradictions became more and more pronounced as the process of liberation became more radicalized.

## Contradictions within the Church

The already existing social tensions in Cuba, in the economic realm, and in the social, cultural, and political realms as well, continued to heighten during that initial phase, since the revolutionary measures and the resistance to them on the part of the minorities who were affected in their long-standing privileges were stirring the people's consciousness. This heightened tension was reflected and made manifest within the church. That had been the case also during the independence struggles of the nineteenth century, although now it was happening in a more obvious way.

In late 1959 and early 1960, the small, privileged sectors affected by the revolutionary measures unfurled their banners against them and against the execution by firing squad of representatives of the overthrown tyranny, those responsible for crimes of repressing the people, and of extremely dangerous counterrevolutionary conspirators. Some Catholic groups went so far as to make use of worship ceremonies to show their solidarity with this stance of hostility to the revolution. These activities immediately ran up against feelings that were being aroused in those sectors of the faithful closest to the heart of the people, and there were protests both inside and outside the church buildings. In some instances police stepped in to settle these clashes, detaining some of those taking part for a few hours. Occasionally these clashes took place on a main street as people came out of church.

At that point there arose a movement called "With Cross and Country," made up of some Catholics who were in sympathy with the revolution. Father Fermán Lence served as their chaplain. This movement took on the defense of the revolution in public ceremonies, and many of its members were involved in the incidents that took place in and around church buildings. The poor esteem in which Father Lence was held and his subsequent public criticism of the Cuban episcopate, which led to his being suspended from exercising his ministry,[8] as well as the extremely antiecclesiastical attitude of some of its members, weakened the movement, and it eventually disappeared.

The counterrevolutionary politicization of some sectors of clergy and laity, which became the dominant note in the church, led the Catholic popular sectors that had directly benefited from the revolution or who adhered to its objectives of social justice to leave the church gradually. These Catholics found it harder and harder to get along in an environment that bristled with hostility at those who had voluntarily enrolled in the militias and had enthusiastically joined up to engage in revolutionary tasks. Many of them found their Christian ideals realized in what the revolution was doing. The church became ever more circumscribed to the most conservative and traditional Catholic groups, since increasingly people from the bourgeoisie, shopkeepers, artisans, and other social sectors unhappy with the revolutionary process, who had not been regular practicing Catholics, began to join up. One explanation for this phenomenon is the fact that the ecclesiastical structure that fitted well into the former society was one of the few that survived the social transformation without undergoing changes.

### The "Counterrevolutionary Pastoral Letters"

The social contradictions reflected within the church, and the growing influence that groups of more conservative Catholics were gaining within it, to the point of almost excluding others, prompted the Cuban bishops to make a public and official expression of their position toward the policies the revolutionary government was developing. The hierarchy based its position on a very conservative interpretation of the social doctrine of the church and thought it was interpreting the feeling of the faithful and even of the whole Cuban people. In fact, without realizing it the hierarchy had been losing contact and solidarity with most of the people.

The Circular Letter of the Cuban Episcopate, dated August 7, 1960, and signed by all the bishops, was sent out with orders that it be read in all churches during Sunday Mass. It declared:

> Social reforms that respect the legitimate rights of all citizens tend to improve the economic, cultural, and social situation of the humble folk; thus they have and always will have the church's unhesitating moral support.
>
> Nevertheless, we would be failing in our obligation to tell you, our faithful, and the people of Cuba in general, all the truth, if in drawing up the balance sheet of the positive and negative aspects of the momentous period our country is experiencing, we should fail to let you know just as clearly our main concerns and fears.
>
> We could indicate some points on which the previously mentioned measures of a social character have not been carried out with due respect for those rights of all citizens that were initially announced, but we believe that it is better for us to focus on an extremely serious problem that no person of good faith can deny at this time, and that is the ever increasing spread of communism in our country.
>
> In recent months the government of Cuba has established close commercial, cultural, and diplomatic relations with the governments of the main communist countries, and especially with the Soviet Union. From a pastoral standpoint we would have nothing to say about the strictly commercial or economic aspects of such growing ties. However, we are indeed deeply disturbed by the fact that in that connection there have been government journalists, labor leaders, and even high government figures who have repeatedly and warmly praised the systems in those countries. In their speeches both in Cuba and elsewhere they have even suggested that there are common points and

analogies in aims and methods between the social revolutions in those countries and the Cuban Revolution. This point concerns us a great deal, since Catholicism and communism follow two totally opposed conceptions of the human being and of the world, views that will never be reconcilable.

Indeed, we condemn communism, first because it is an essentially materialistic and atheistic doctrine and because governments guided by it are among the worst enemies the church and humanity have ever known throughout history. Deceitfully claiming that they have utter respect for all religions, in every country they gradually destroy all the church's social, charitable, educational, and apostolic activities, and they disrupt it from within, by jailing the most zealous and active bishops and priests, under the most varied pretexts.

We also condemn communism because it is a system that brutually denies the most fundamental rights of the human person; because in order to achieve total state control over the means of production, it always sets up a dictatorial regime in which a small group uses police terror to set itself over the rest of the citizenry; because it completely dominates the political economy, often sacrificing the welfare of the people to the ambitions and convenience of the ruling group; because it gradually does away with the right of property, and over the long run turns all citizens, not even into employees, but into true slaves of the state; because it denies to the people their right to know the truth, since the state becomes the owner of all the media and does not allow all the citizens access to opinions different from those maintained by the ruling group; because it wrongfully subordinates the life of the family to the state, pressuring the woman to leave the home to do very harsh jobs outside the home, and educating the children according to the government's desires, without rightly taking into account the will of the parents.

In condemning communist doctrines and methods, therefore, the church does not do so in a one-sided way in

> the name of particular groups in society that might be affected by the establishment of a regime of this nature; it does so in the name of the inalienable rights of all people, which in one way or another are unscrupulously violated by communist governments.
>
> Recall, dear children, and say it aloud to all of Cuba, that the church is not afraid of deep social reforms as long as they are based on justice and charity, for they seek the people's welfare and the church rejoices in that. However, it is just for that reason, because it loves the people and desires their welfare, that the church cannot refrain from condemning communist doctrines. Today the church stands on the side of the humble and will always stand there, but it does not, nor will it ever, stand on the side of communism.[9]

Alluding directly to the frequent appeals for the unity of the whole population made by the revolutionary government in view of the increasing threats and aggressions of the United States government and its local agents, and alluding also to the invitations Fidel Castro himself was making to Catholics as a whole, and especially to Catholic women, to join in revolutionary work in society, the bishops end their letter with these words:

> Let no one in the name of any misunderstood united citizenry urge us Catholics to muffle our opposition to these teachings, for we could not do so without betraying our fundamental principles. The vast majority of the Cuban people, who are Catholics, stand opposed to materialistic and atheistic communism, and they could be led into a communist regime only through deceit and coercion. May the Most Blessed Virgin of Charity not allow this ever to happen in Cuba.
>
> Thus we pray to God Our Lord through the intercession of our Supreme Patroness.[10]

This pastoral stance adopted toward the policies developed by the revolutionary government simply echoed the doctrinal posture of the universal church toward communism during that period. Many Catholics used it to try to justify their counterrevolutionary activities. All of that left a deep imprint on the attitude of the church and toward the church in Cuba for years afterward.

## The Church and Urban Reform

Similar to the agrarian reform, the constitutional law of urban reform, decreed on October 14, 1960, limited ownership of urban housing units to the one occupied by the owner or the owner's family, and permitted ownership of a second house only in a recreational area; all other properties were expropriated. This enabled former renters or legal occupants of houses in cities and towns to acquire the house in which they had been living by amortizing the price by means of their former rents. The price for the expropriation was set in inverse proportion to the age of the building and in direct proportion to the value the previous owner had declared for property-tax purposes. This measure affected the minority of former landlords just as it benefited the vast majority of the population, who became owners of their own homes.

The institutional church and many religious orders had significant investments in this area of the economy and their income was affected like that of other urban landlords. Some tried to present this revolutionary measure as a direct attack on the church and on the economic independence needed to carry out its apostolate. The landlord philosophy guiding the church's social behavior unquestionably prevented it from understanding and putting trust in ways of solving its material needs that would be smoother and less compromising of its principles than capitalist investment, which it had itself previously condemned.

This urban reform was the first major impact on the church's economy, contrary to the case of the local bourgeoisie, which had already been affected by the agrarian reform.

## The Death of Bishop Martín Villaverde of Matanzas

On November 3, 1960, Bishop Alberto Martín Villaverde of Matanzas died. A man of extraordinary piety and gospel meekness, he was very much loved and respected in his diocese.

His funeral was celebrated with solemnity in the cathedral church of Matanzas, with a large number of people from the diocese in attendance as well as ecclesiastical and lay leaders from the other dioceses. The large funeral procession left the cathedral and made its way around the city on foot, bearing his remains to the cemetery, which was located at the edge of the city. Not only did the government not prohibit the funeral, but the traffic police provided assistance.

When the ceremony was over, Bishop Boza Masvidal bade farewell to the people with fiery words of mourning, and explicit references to the rights of the church, which he said were threatened by the revolution.

Bishop Martín Villaverde was succeeded in the see of Matanzas by Bishop José Maximino Domínguez who, like Bishop Boza Masvidal, was an auxiliary bishop of Havana.

## The Social Behavior of Catholics

As the church's political line was made explicit, both in the official statements made by the bishops from their pastoral positions and by the clergy out of their ideological starting points, the faithful reacted in a variety of ways, which went in two basic directions.

Most of the believers, who had a deep-seated Afro-Catholic religious syncretism, immediately felt the benefit of the revolutionary measures and they quickly became involved in the mass organizations created by the revolution to speed popular mobilization and participation in revolutionary activity. However, the privileged minorities and the sectors culturally and ideologically controlled by those who reacted against the revolution became ever more decisively the basis of the church's organizational and financial support, and their influence on its pastoral direction continued to grow.

In addition, the ideology underlying the church's social doctrine, in combination with the general mode of life of the clergy, heightened the class difference among Catholics and hastened the desertion of the church by popular sectors and the divorce between the church and the people. The fact that the hierarchy and the clergy were out of contact with the people prevented the church from grasping the changes that were taking place in the social and individual consciousness of the people, and led them to explain the fact that people were leaving the church as due to a deception or coercion. However, the only people who believed that explanation were those who went to church to seek spiritual refuge because they lacked a faith that could nourish their social commitment.

The fact that the church was stuck in the most conservative remnants of society and that those remnants took refuge in it meant that church organizations and properties could be used by counterrevolutionary movements for conspiring even more widely and intensively than they had previously been used to support the revolutionary struggle against the deposed tyranny. Catholic schools, parish catechetical centers, religious houses, churches, and ecclesiastical meeting places were used by a number of priests and lay people for conspiring against the revolution to a greater or lesser extent.

When some counterrevolutionary conspiratorial networks were broken and those caught were jailed and sentenced, it was clear that some of these movements, by now manipulated from outside, were headed by well-known former Catholic leaders. Such facts prompted various popular and political reactions against the church and its members, which translated into frequent arrests of catechists and lay leaders. The fact that such arrests were brief did not make them less unjust or coercive.

At this point there also occurred an incident outside the church, which nevertheless had regrettable repercussions in and for the church. During a television appearance by the prime minister, Fidel Castro, the Spanish ambassador, Juan Pablo de Lojendio, went into a vulgar and uncontrolled outburst, violating all norms of diplomatic behavior, and had to be taken away by force. Surprisingly, a few days later a group of superiors of religious orders in Cuba, all of them Spanish citizens, without obtaining or even seeking the permission of the hierarchy, wrote a letter expressing solidarity and support to the ambassador for his action. In the letter they also expressed their sympathy for Francisco Franco, then head of state in Spain. The strictly political nature of this action, taken without consultation by these highly visible Spanish religious, led Archbishop Evelio

Díaz of Havana personally to disavow and condemn it. However, that was not enough to prevent a strong reaction, not just against those responsible but against the church itself, on the part of official sectors in the state as well as among broad sectors of the population. Consequently the atmosphere became even more tense.

The last publicly visible conciliatory gesture was that of Bishop Evelio Díaz Cía, then coadjutor archbishop of Havana with right of succession, when with a personal invitation he attended the large Martí Banquet organized by the revolutionary government for the people on the night of January 27, 1960, the eve of the birth date of José Martí, a national hero. Bishop Evelio dined with Fidel Castro at the presidential table. The celebration was broadcast on national television and the public could witness the frequent conversation between the bishop and Castro as they dined. Bishop Evelio was quickly criticized by influential Catholics who had turned against the revolution.

The sharp contradictions that unfolded during this first phase continued to grow until they gave way to a second phase in the relations between the Catholic church and the revolutionary Cuban state, that of confrontation.

# 3

# Confrontation (1961–1962)

The Catholic community in Cuba was especially vulnerable to counterrevolutionary propaganda campaigns run from outside the country. The one that most frightened a large segment of Cuban Catholics was the campaign accusing the revolutionary government of planning to pry children away from the moral and educational guardianship of their parents. Most of the Spanish clergy and religious in Cuba, who were sympathizers of the "Catholic" Franco regime, then ruling Spain with the acquiescence of the top leadership of the Spanish church, supported these campaigns, which utilized testimonies to the effect that large numbers of Spanish children had been sent "to Russia" during the Spanish Civil War. That fact, plus a vast abundance of printed anticommunist literature then circulating among Cuban Catholics, swelled even more the ranks of Catholics emigrating to Spain and the United States.

Among the ranks of those leaving Cuba there were large numbers of children unaccompanied by their parents. The parents were encouraged to send their children abroad by teaching religious orders, which even provided transportation and offered scholarships in cooperation with their mother houses in Spain and with Catholic Welfare Services in the United States. Meanwhile the parents stayed behind to hold onto their property and belongings, waiting for the government to be overthrown by the United States government or armed forces.

The widening gap between the Cuban Catholic community and the rest of the population, in conjunction with the phenomenon of migration among its members, led to a strange attitude: in general, the church began to be more concerned about "saving" its members from communism by helping them to emigrate than about carrying out a mission to the society of which it was a part. As a result the Cuban church gradually acquired more bonds with Catholic exile communities than with Cuba, its own country. The Cuban church began "to have its feet in Cuba but its mind and heart in Miami or Madrid"; it was becoming a foreigner in its own country.

As a result the church's apostolic mission was utterly nullified; at the same time the counterrevolutionary militancy of the most conservative Cuban Catholics still in the country became even more pronounced. They hoped to pave the way for the fall of the revolutionary government through action from outside as a practical way of being reunited with their relatives who had emigrated without losing their possessions in Cuba.

The encouragement and aid the Catholic clergy offered so that Cubans could leave the country drew to the church many people who had no liking for the revolution. Such people began to call themselves Catholics and attend worship in order to get papers to leave the country, even though many of them had never been in the habit of going to church. Thus was created the mirage that the church was growing and becoming stronger in Cuba despite the emigration and alleged persecution it was suffering. That exacerbated the church's triumphalism and encouraged its use as a counterrevolutionary political force.

Religious networks were widely used to bring into the country and distribute anticommunist and counterrevolutionary literature. "News" from the CIA-sponsored Radio Swan and the Station of the Americas and from the Voice of America, the ideological mouthpiece of the United States government, was standard fare in Catholic churches, schools, and religious houses.

The Catholic University (Santo Tomás de Villanueva), then headed by Auxiliary Bishop Eduardo Boza Masvidal, became a center of opposition and conspiracy on the part of well-off students, as did many Catholic schools. This took place after some Catholic leaders failed in their attempt to become part of the leadership of the University Student Federation (FEU) of the University of Havana in order to prevent this traditionally combative institution of Cuban students from becoming fully a part of the revolution.

Bishop Boza Masvidal was not only a bishop and university rector, but also pastor of Our Lady of Charity Church in Havana, the archdiocesan shrine. With the help of some priests and religious he organized an "information network," supposedly to make up for the lack of Catholic media, in order to call the flock to worship services and to inform them about other church-connected activities. This network was organized into four branches, each named after one of the evangelists. The head of each branch was in direct contact with Bishop Boza and with four other members, and each of these had four others, and so it continued.

Influencing this stage of confrontation were some events prior to 1961, such as the departure of the former leader of the Catholic University Group, Manuel Artime, who had joined the Rebel Army just a few days before the revolutionary victory. Relieved of his job as the head of a zone of agricultural development, he left the country and joined the counterrevolutionary groups operating out of the United States and preparing to invade the island. Other developments during this stage of confrontation were the resignation of some Catholic leaders who had administrative posts in the revolutionary government, such as Dr. Andrés Valdespino, the undersecretary of the treasury; the involvement of many Catholic leaders in counterrevolutionary movements in the country, such as the Movement to Recover the Revolution (MRR) and the Revolutionary People's Movement (MRP); and the often unjustified seeking of asylum in foreign embassies on the part of several leaders of the Young Catholic Workers (JOC), Young Catholic Students (JEC), and Catholic University Youth (JUC), as well as the arrest of others and their trial and sentencing at the hands of the revolutionary courts.

## Repercussions of the Bay of Pigs

The failed attempt by the United States to overthrow the Cuban Revolution militarily through the use of counterrevolutionaries contracted outside the country was a dramatic moment for the history of the church in Cuba, since it led the revolution to define itself as socialist. The church had already publicly declared its opposition to socialism, and a large proportion of practicing Catholics was sympathetic to a "liberation" that might come by way of the North American government. Notable figures in the Catholic hierarchy, clergy and laity, participated in, or at least indirectly supported, some of the counterrevolutionary movements that claimed to be defending "Western, Christian, democratic" society.

At the start of the invasion, the country's armed forces, aided by the popular militia and the Committees to Defend the Revolution, quickly rounded up many individuals who were suspected of being dangerously sympathetic to the invaders. Militia units occupied most of the church's buildings while this state of war prevailed, although there was never any order to suspend worship. Nevertheless, in many churches worship services were suspended because priests and the faithful were afraid or did not show up.

All the bishops of Cuba were put under house arrest in their episcopal residences, except for Bishops Evelio Díaz and Boza Masvidal, who were held in the offices of the Department of State Security for several days.

There were three Catholic chaplains in the attacking military force: Father Ismael Lugo, a Capuchin; Tomás Macho, a Jesuit; and Segundo de las Horas, a Pious School priest. These three were captured with the other survivors of the invasion, and they were shown on television along with the other members of the brigade. Heading the expedition as its political chief was Manuel Artime Buesa, formerly a Catholic leader.

The invasion was defeated in sixty-eight hours, and things quickly returned to normal, but the fact that highly visible Catholics had been involved in this act of aggression did nothing to raise the esteem of the church or arouse any sympathy for it among the Cuban people. The already existing antagonism between Catholics who were disenchanted with the revolution and the rest of the population grew. Campaigns against the revolution, in Catholic schools and agencies, were stepped up with the hope that that would stimulate a direct and decisive action from the United States; at the same time mistrust of Cuban revolutionaries toward anything Catholic was also accentuated, and indeed in an indiscriminate manner.

The passions surrounding and accentuating contradictions translated immediately into more people leaving the church and into an increase in the numbers of the Catholic faithful who left the country.[1]

In order to grant visas to those who wanted to leave, the Spanish embassy required letters of recommendation from Catholic priests, instead of the commercial guarantees they had previously required. The priests, who in their own consciences might have very diverse reasons, were forced to be involved in this awkward procedure for several years until the Cuban bishops managed to persaude the Spanish authorities not to insist on this requirement.

## The Nationalization of Education

The law of June 6, 1961, which made education public and free, declared that all schools were nationalized. The measure affected all private schools, including church schools, which were traditionally one of its main sources of income and means of catechetical instruction.

Parish catechesis in Cuba was not ready to take on the religious formation of Catholic children. At that time there was practically no catechesis in the family or for adults or prior to the sacraments, and thus the nationalization of private schools left the church extremely unprepared to carry out its catechetical function.

After the schools were nationalized, the members of religious orders, especially those devoted to teaching, left in large numbers. They took up their educational activities in other Latin American countries and even in the United States. There was also a significant increase in the exodus of Catholic families with their children. A notable exception to this process of emigration of members of religious orders was the decision of the Jesuits to leave a group in Cuba. They offered themselves to the bishops, primarily to do pastoral work. Some religious orders left only a few members, usually older people, in order to hold onto their buildings.

The measure did not affect the major seminary in Havana or the minor seminary in Santiago de Cuba, but the Matanzas seminary closed for lack of teachers. Something similar took place with the novitiates of religious orders, although some of them were occupied during the Bay of Pigs invasion and have never been returned. On the other hand, others, especially women's orders, have continued to operate and have even increased their enrollment (for example, the Daughters of Charity).

## Money Exchange

The fact that the rich and privileged had taken large sums of money out of circulation in order to hoard it, use it in the black market, or finance counterrevolutionary movements, and that some foreign embassies were supporting such criminal actions was dragging down the country's economy. Laws against the crimes of hoarding, unlawful trading, and counterrevolution were instituted, but it was hard to limit such activity by these normal means.

Law number 963, decreed August 4, 1961, invalidated all currency in circulation and provided for it to be turned in for exchange in reasonable amounts on Monday, August 7. Families were allowed to have up to 10,000 pesos, with 200 given immediately and 1,000 shortly afterward, and the remainder deposited in special bank accounts. Foreign embassies could trade an unlimited amount, with the approval of the Foreign Ministry. Amounts deposited in bank accounts were exchanged in their entirety.

This measure had a big impact on the financial capability of the counterrevolution, but indirectly it also affected the economic resources of the church. Bishops, religious orders, and Catholic organizations were holding onto large sums of money, which they did not deposit in banks because they did not trust the national banking system. In his memoirs, Father Hilario Chaurrondo, C.M.,[2] says that when he was in the nunciature he was surprised to see the huge sums of money that bishops, priests, religious-order members, and wealthy lay people took there so that the chargé d'affaires could change it, thus taking advantage of his diplomatic privileges. The amount of money involved was so great that Archbishop Zacchi refused to do it, saying that it would be a scandal and would damage the church's reputation.

## The Taking Over of the Cristóbal Colón Cemetery

The socialization of public services included the turning over to the municipal government of the Colón Cemetery of the city of Havana on August 4, 1963. The largest and most important cemetery in Cuba, it had been created by the bishop of Havana, beginning in 1862, on the church's own lands and had been administered by the church through a government concession.

This 1963 resolution was decreed at a time when the church-state clash was most intense. The basis for the decree was the supposed "profit-making nature" with which the church administered its burial services. Even though an old but still valid law from the republican period had declared that administrative concessions of public services to private citizens was invalid, this routine reason for legally terminating the administrative concession to the church of this public service was, inexplicably, not put forward.

The church used judicial procedures to protest not so much the measure itself as the reason put forth, since it was carrying out this function in accordance with the rates officially approved by the municipal government itself. The matter ended when the measure was ratified by the Supreme Court. Throughout this process, the church's right to celebrate religious worship in the cemetery was upheld, both in the main chapel and beside the gravestones.

Under public administration, funeral services were made free, the area was expanded, all the pathways were repaired, and the whole area was kept up and embellished. The church would not have been able to pay for such things.

## *La Caridad* Procession

During the most tense moments in relations between the church and the revolutionary state, Bishop Eduardo Boza Masvidal, an auxiliary in Havana and in charge of the parish of Our Lady of Charity there, which was the diocesan shrine for the Patroness of Cuba, organized an interparochial mass gathering and procession to honor the Holy Patroness. The plan was to march from the parish church to the cathedral on Sunday, September 10, 1961. In previous years this procession had never gone beyond the vicinity of the shrine, and only the local parishioners took part. Both revolutionary and counterrevolutionary circles interpreted the change as an attempt at a public display of political strength.

In compliance with laws dealing with such matters, which had been in effect since Spanish colonial times, the pastor sought permission from civil and police authorities. Utilizing his cell-based "news network," he mobilized all the parishes and Catholic organizations in the diocese. On Sunday the 10th, a delegation from the parish confraternity went to the police station to inquire about the permission. They were advised to cancel the event in view of the angry reactions that might break out. However, the permission was in fact given, and at three o'clock in the afternoon thousands of Catholics and people disenchanted with the revolution filled the church and the surrounding streets.

Things were very confused in the crowd, and there were disagreements and hesitations due to the contradictory reports circulating. Some said permission had been denied as a way of repressing the church's rights; some said Bishop Boza had decided not to hold the procession; others said the permission had been delayed but finally obtained; still others said the procession would go forward no matter what. At four o'clock in the afternoon there were cries to begin the march, and thus began a disorderly movement toward the cathedral.

This unusual demonstration had prompted a parallel gathering of hundreds of citizens who were shouting insults at the marchers and accusing them of being counterrevolutionaries. The head of the procession had gone only a few blocks when shots were heard and there was a rumor that someone had been wounded. The police soon appeared on the scene and ordered the marchers to disband, and in fact they were already scattering because of the shots.

The death of Arnaldo Socorro, the young man who had been hit by the shots, led to a police investigation that implicated several Catholic leaders, who were tried for an illegal demonstration and homicide. Some were punished with jail sentences of varying lengths. The version that appeared in the revolutionary media was that the shots had come from the church bell tower, something that the church always denied.

The incident heightened tensions even more and had its impact on those Catholics who professed their faith and yet were sympathetic to the revolution. On the one hand, ordinary people left the church in larger numbers and, on the other hand, the counterrevolutionary position of Catholics against the revolution hardened even more. From that point onward, Bishop Boza was held up as a symbol of counterrevolutionary movements both inside and outside the country.

## The Expulsion of Priests from Cuba

The very day Socorro was buried the Ministry of the Interior released a statement denouncing the fact that the Catholic church was being used by the enemies of the people in order to conspire against the revolution, with the complicity of some high-level clerics.

On the following day, September 12, an operation to arrest priests began throughout the island. Under police custody they were brought to the Spanish ship *Covadonga.* On September 17 the ship left the port of Havana with 132 Catholic priests on board. Most of those expelled were Spaniards, although the group included Cubans, among them Bishop Eduardo Boza Masvidal.

For the most part the group was made up of priests who in some fashion had been engaged in political activity against the revolution or the measures it had carried out. There were, however, exceptions, as was proved by the fact that some of them later returned to Cuba, including Father Francisco Oves Fernández, who later became archbishop of Havana.

This operation broke up for good any counterrevolutionary political organization that might have taken shape within the Cuban Catholic church. The number of clergy in the country declined even more and, as a result, those Catholics who were disenchanted with the revolution became even more fearful. They joined the lines of those who were trying to leave the country for good, and thus the number of practicing Catholics in Cuba further declined.

It should be pointed out that, with the departure from Cuba of this body of priests and the previous voluntary departure of priests, the clergy now numbered 200—in comparison with the 800 priests present before the revolutionary victory. Taking these figures into account, and factoring in those who had died and those newly ordained, leads to a conclusion that, by their own decision, about 460 pastors abandoned their flock in Cuba during these three years.

This event marks the approximate end of the period of sharp and direct confrontation between the church and the Cuban Revolution. The distinguishing feature of the phase that now opens is that of people leaving the country: the large-scale departure of Catholics. This is the phase of flight.

# 4

# Flight (1963–1967)

As 1963 began, the Catholic church in Cuba was suffering setbacks in all respects.

There were six bishops, all heading dioceses. The diocesan clergy was reduced to one-fourth of what it had been in 1958, more than half having left the country on their own. The few seminarians who returned to Cuba after finishing their studies elsewhere could not make up for their brethren who had deserted their homeland. Religious orders were even more affected by the fact that almost all the teaching orders and many of the rest abandoned their mission territories. Women's religious orders numbered only fourteen, with very few members left in Cuba. In most of them, only a few elderly sisters remained in the country, occupying their large convents to prevent their being nationalized or "diocesanized."

Only the two largest diocesan seminaries remained in operation: El Buen Pastor (Good Shepherd) in Havana and San Basilio (St. Basil) in Santiago de Cuba, both of which were put at the service of all the dioceses. Religious-order novitiates practically disappeared, in some cases because they were occupied by the government and in others because there were no staff and no vocations. Men's religious orders began to send their few new novices to diocesan seminaries. At the end of their studies the novices added a period of training in the rule of the order and the discipline maintained in their religious houses. Something similar took place with the women's orders, except for the Daughters of Charity, who continued to work in different types of care (hospitals, old people's homes, and so forth) and had a substantial number of novices.

Lay associations, congregations, and confraternities began to find it difficult to follow their own rules, due to lack of membership. Many practically disappeared and others lost their juridical independence and reverted to being legally under the church itself. That was also true of some religious orders.

Worship went into a drastic decline. City churches, where six or eight Sunday Masses had formerly been celebrated, cut the number to two or three, so the priests could provide services for other nearby communities. In rural parishes Mass was celebrated only weekly or biweekly, since the pastor was taking care of three, four, or even five adjoining parishes.

The fewer numbers of clergy gave lay people active in Catholic Action and the organizations composing it a much greater weight in the church's pastoral work. That role was more in tune with the renewed participation in the church that Vatican Council II was acknowledging for the laity. Nevertheless, this new lay participation, in view of the precarious situation of the clergy in Cuba, led to a new kind of clericalization of the laity (neoclericalism) insofar as the laity took on ecclesiastical responsibilities that took them away, or at least distracted them, from the secular responsibilities proper to their state. In practice, the lay people most ready to take on these quasi-clerical functions were those who were getting ready to leave the country for good, and were giving up their secular work while waiting for the day they could leave. They took refuge in ecclesiastical tasks as a way of passing the time, to avoid collaborating with the revolution and to enhance their ideological position outside the country. Thus it was that a good deal of the church community remained bodily in Cuba, but with heart and mind elsewhere.

## The Death of Cardinal Arteaga

On March 20, 1963, His Eminence Cardinal Manuel Arteaga Betancourt of Havana, the only Cuban raised to the rank of cardinal, died at an advanced age after a prolonged illness.

Although he was much criticized and attacked throughout his life as a bishop, Cardinal Arteaga was one of the Cuban bishops who did the most to further the promotion of Cuban-born clergy to high church leadership. Because he became increasingly senile during his later years, some of his relatives, friends, and subordinates were able to carry out administrative actions on their own which were quite foreign to the cardinal's nature and did nothing to enhance the church's public image. The 1959 appointment of Bishop Evelio Díaz Cía as assistant (or coadjutor) archbishop with right of succession was a wise move on the part of the Holy See. From November 14, 1959 onward, Bishop Evelio took charge of pastoral care in the archdiocese of the capital city, while the cardinal went to live at the residence of the ambassador of Argentina until that country broke relations with Cuba. Subsequently the brothers of San Juan de Dios took care of him in San Rafael Clinic, until his death, which came not unexpectedly. All the bishops in the country and many of the faithful from all spheres of the church attended his funeral services both in the cathedral and in the cemetery.

The cardinal's departure did not bring any substantial change in the makeup and pastoral direction of the archdiocese, which Bishop Evelio Díaz Cía had been administering for some time. Nor was there any change in the Cuban church, which has not been honored with another cardinal since that time.

## The Release of Four Priests from Prison

On the day (March 21) that Cardinal Arteaga was buried, the only priests in prison for counterrevolutionary activities were freed and brought from the Isle of Pines to Havana. One was a Cuban, Reinerio Lebroc, and three were Spaniards, Francisco López Blázquez, Ramón Fidalgo, and Luis Rojo. They were turned over to the papal nunciature, where they remained for a few days until they left the country.

Some priests had escaped being arrested, tried, and sentenced by taking asylum in the embassies of Latin American governments, while others remained in Cuba after giving up their counterrevolutionary activities. The Cuban government was releasing the only Catholic priests in custody for political reasons, since the three who were part of the invading force at the Bay of Pigs were already gone from the country. The Cuban government had arranged with the United States to trade them and the rest of the invaders for food and medicine.

Still remaining behind, however, were Catholic lay people involved in counterrevolutionary activities, sometimes at the instigation of their ecclesiastical advisers. These lay people did have to face the full rigor of the courts.

## The Return of Cuban Priests and the Entry of Foreign Clergy

During this phase several young priests returned to Cuba after being ordained in Rome. They had been among the seminarians sent by their bishops to finish their studies shortly after the revolutionary victory or, later, as a result of the temporary closing of the seminaries by the hierarchy after the Bay of Pigs invasion.

Similarly, government authorities allowed several priests from among the 132 expelled in 1961 to return. Some of those returning were Cubans, such as Father Francisco Oves Fernández, who was later promoted to head the see of Havana. There were also foreigners who had exercised their ministry in Cuba for years.

Through the efforts of the papal nunciature some foreign missionaries were allowed to come to the country with temporary residency permits. Among them were eight Belgian priests who were assigned to the dioceses of Camagüey, the one most lacking clergy at that time.

Things did not work out well for these Belgian priests. Even more than other foreign priests they failed to grasp adequately the peculiar features of the church or the people in Cuba. Because of their relative numbers in comparison to the few in the diocese of Camagüey, plus the fact that they were better informed about the council and could more easily import books and other things, they dominated pastoral matters in the diocese. Thus they could give that work direction without taking into account the traditions of the country or the political context in which the church found itself. They urged that Catholics be more involved in the labor organizations and social organizations in the country. However, since these Catholics had not understood or accepted the political direction of the revolution, their urging led to conflict situations in several cases. Due to their influence and that of the few Cuban and young priests in the area, the pastoral and organizational direction of the diocese of Camagüey differed considerably from that of the other dioceses.

When these missionaries left Cuba after the expiration and nonrenewal of their residency permits, some Catholics who followed them were involved in conspiratorial activities. When they were caught they were sent to prison, and that had further consequences for the church.

Incidents like these were probably what prompted the revolutionary authorities shortly afterward to prohibit the arrival of other foreign missionaries or exiled Cubans and to suggest that priestly vocations be stimulated in Cuba. Cuban youth would have a better understanding of the people and the revolution than any foreigner.

Nevertheless, in subsequent years various groups of foreign sisters were allowed to come and live in Cuba in order to strengthen the apostolic and socially useful work of their orders.

## The Appointment of New Auxiliary Bishops for Havana

With the appointment of Bishop José Maximino Domínguez to head the diocese of Matanzas, the archdiocese of Havana had been left without auxiliary bishops. Perhaps because this capital-city archdiocese had almost half of the clergy and because of the variety of religious orders present, it was the hardest diocese to administer.

On March 28, 1964, the Holy See made a diocesan priest, Father Alfredo Llaguno y Canals, and a Jesuit, Father Fernando Azcárate y Freire de Andrade, auxiliary bishops of the archdiocese. They were consecrated in the cathedral on May 17 with a large number of the faithful present, filling the church, the courtyard, and a good deal of the adjacent plaza. Both bishops were auxiliaries in Havana until 1970 when Archbishop Díaz Cía's request for a replacement was accepted and the Holy See assigned Bishop Oves to succeed him in the archdiocesan see.

The incoming archbishop had no auxiliaries at that point; he entrusted the pastoral care of the diocese to his vicars, and assigned Bishop Azcárate to take care of the central parish of Our Lady of Monserrate. He kept Bishop Llaguno in charge of his old parish and the hospital of San Francisco de Paula. Later, Bishop Evelio Ramos, previously rector of El Buen Pastor Seminary, was made auxiliary bishop.[1]

## The Death of Pope John XXIII and the Election of Paul VI

Reactions in Cuba to the death of the beloved Pope John XXIII were similar to those in other countries, although they were less intense due to the isolation of the Cuban church. In the metropolitan cathedral church of Havana solemn funeral honors were presided over by the chargé d'affaires of the Holy See, Bishop Cesare Zacchi. There were similar celebrations in the other cathedrals and in many parishes as well. The revolutionary government decreed three days of official mourning throughout the country for the death of the head of the Vatican State, with which the republic of Cuba maintained, and still maintains, relations.

However, the general reaction of the Catholic people was not so emotional, nor so widespread, as in other countries. More conservative sectors in the church, hoping that the bark of Peter would get a pilot who would steer it through less stormy seas, yearned for a new Pius XII. Sectors more committed to renewal, and especially those most integrated into their society, trusted that the new successor of Peter would continue and deepen the pastoral lines undertaken by the amazing Pope Roncalli.

John XXIII's encyclicals *Mater et Magistra* and *Pacem in Terris* had been studied only in tiny circles of priests, in seminaries, and in groups of lay leaders. The reactions produced varied according to the ideological positions of the members. Not until the end of Vatican II, two years later, were these papal documents incorporated into the study of both the conciliar documents and the encyclicals of Pope Paul VI among wider circles of Catholics.

The election of Paul VI was disturbing to those who trusted that John XXIII's death would end the "adventure" into which this Holy Father had launched the universal church. However, it was encouraging to the more progressive groups within Cuban Catholicism. Cardinal Montini had a reputation as a cultivated, realistic, and progressive man, and he gave reason to believe that the windows opened by his predecessor would not be closed and that he would open even more windows, as in fact he did as long as his health permitted.

## The Resignation and Replacement of Bishop Riú Anglés

Bishop Carlos Riú Anglés, a Spaniard, had been appointed bishop of Camagüey in 1948 to replace Bishop Enrique Pérez Serantes, when the latter took over the archdiocese of Santiago de Cuba. The piety shown by the new bishop in Camagüey during his earlier years as pastor of Banes led people to believe that he would be an outstanding bishop.

However, the marked contrast between the exceeding modesty and hesitancy of the new bishop and the flamboyant oratory and activity of his predecessor were too abrupt a change. Bishop Riú never thought that the people of Camagüey accepted him as they had his predecessor and as he had expected they would him. Consequently he became more withdrawn within his episcopal residence and among the small circle of priests and friends closest to him. The radical changes brought about by the revolution made the bishop even more withdrawn. His feelings of failure and his illnesses, normal for his age, convinced him not to return to Cuba after he attended the first session of Vatican II in 1962. He petitioned the Holy See to replace him and allow him to return to Spain. There he lived in retirement and prayer. He then moved to the United States, where he lived until his death.

On September 10, 1964, Bishop Riú's resignation was accepted by the Holy See, and Father Adolfo Rodríguez Herrera was chosen to succeed him. While a pastor in the diocese he had been made auxiliary bishop of the diocese and was in charge of its administration during Bishop Riú's absence. Bishop Adolfo Rodríguez had to confront the difficult situation in which the diocese had been left.

## The Death of Father Sardiñas

Father Guillermo Sardiñas, of the archdiocese of Havana, was the only priest who fully, decisively, and publicly took part in the Cuban Revolution. In no way did that affect his faith or his loyalty to the church.

During the struggle for liberation in the mountains of Cuba, Father Sardiñas joined the Rebel Army led by Fidel Castro and there exercised his priestly ministry as chaplain to Catholic believers involved in the guerrilla war and as a missionary in those remote regions, where he baptized many peasants in accordance with the customary mission style of that period. Before the victory of the people's rebellion, the High Command of the Rebel Army conferred on him the rank of *comandante.*

When the liberation struggle achieved victory, Father Sardiñas returned to pastoral work in the archdiocese of Havana as pastor of the new parish of Cristo Rey (Christ the King). For its temporary church the parish used the meeting place of Branch A of Cuban Catholic Action. Sardiñas was not discharged from the Rebel Army, however, as evidenced by the fact that he went around in public in his strange uniform, an olive-green cassock bearing his military honors. This prompted many of the Havana priests to reject Father Sardiñas during the first few years of the revolution, even though the archbishop repeatedly and publicly acknowledged Sardiñas's fidelity to the church.

On December 21, 1964, Father Sardiñas died after a brief illness, still wholly dedicated to the church. His burial attracted major church leaders from the diocese and outstanding revolutionary figures, despite the fact that it took place at the same time as the funeral of André Voisin (a French scientist who devoted his final years to agricultural research and work, and to teaching in Cuba), whose funeral was huge. At Father Sardiñas's funeral the Catholic liturgy was combined with the official honors given by the state for a soldier killed in action.

## The Influence of Vatican Council II

In Rome this was the period of Vatican Council II, which was opened by John XXIII and closed by Paul VI. This extremely important event went almost unnoticed by the Cuban church, which was immersed in its own very specific tensions and concerns. That was especially true of the faithful, who heard only sporadic information on the changes wrought by the council. Many of them interpreted the changes in their own fashion, sometimes attributing them to the pressures or exigencies of the revolutionary process taking place in their own country.

Attending various sessions of the council from Cuba were Bishops José Maximino Domínguez of Matanzas who was then the secretary of the Bishops Conference of Cuba, Fernando Azcárate, auxiliary in Havana, Adolfo Rodríguez Herrera of Camagüey, and Manuel Rodríguez Rozas of Pinar del Río. Upon returning from the sessions they attended, all of them traveled around in order to be available for discussions and conferences in parishes, centers of the apostolates, and religious houses in their dioceses, striving to make known the basic outlines of the renewal of the church that the council proposed.

Even before the council ended on December 8, 1965, the impact of the ecclesial reflection launched by the council began to make itself felt hesitantly in the Cuban church. The first changes were in the liturgy. There was little opposition from the regular churchgoers, but the changes were not very substantial. A very important change, both immediately and in the long run, was the reform of seminary discipline, which began in El Buen Pastor Seminary at the initiative of the rector, Father Carlos Manuel de Céspedes. The subsequent transfer of this diocesan seminary to the magnificent historical building of the former San Carlos Seminary in Old Havana made an indirect but useful contribution to this modernization of discipline.

In addition the peculiar circumstances of the church in Cuba and of Cuban society persuaded the bishops to undertake a radical restructuring of the lay apostolate by disbanding Catholic Action. They also introduced some new ecclesiastical structures recommended by the council, such as bishops commissions, priests councils, and zone vicariates. Nevertheless, it was only a little later that the hierarchy approved of and adopted an ecumenical stance toward other Christian churches. There were efforts to dialogue with nonbelievers, such as those carried out personally by Father Carlos M. de Céspedes, and some even through the press, but these efforts ran up against the incomprehension of many in the church and were blocked. Institutionally speaking, the pastoral impulse behind such relations was timid, hesitant, and very limited. Moreover, political circles, which were still filled with mistrust and limitations in both theory and practice, did not welcome or encourage such efforts.

## Father Loredo's Arrest and Conviction

On April 11, 1966, a regrettable incident took place that led to the arrest of two priests and a Franciscan lay brother; one of them, young Father Miguel Angel Loredo, was sentenced to fifteen years' imprisonment.

A few days before, a man trying to leave the country illegally attempted to hijack a commercial passenger plane belonging to Cuban Air Lines and to force it to fly to the United States. Instead of going to Miami, the pilot returned to Cuba without the hijacker noticing. When he realized the trick and saw that he was once more back in Cuba, he fired his weapon killing one crew member. After escaping and being hunted by the police for several days, he was finally arrested. The authorities found that the religious who lived in the San Francisco district of Old Havana had been involved in hiding him.

Subsequently the legal investigation led to the release of both Father Serafín Ajuria, O.F.M., the Franciscan superior in Cuba, and the porter of the religious house. Both were later absolved of the accusations. That was not the case with Father Loredo, however, who was held under preventive arrest from the beginning and then was sentenced to prison for having helped hide the fugitive.

During his years in prison, Father Loredo exercised his priestly ministry among the prisoners, completely sharing in their situation because of his repeated refusal to be involved in rehabilitation programs. In Feburary 1976 Father Loredo was conditionally released, even though he had not served his whole fifteen-year sentence, which would have ended in 1981. Archbishop Zacchi had arranged for his release from prison, which, however, took place several months after the end of Zacchi's term as papal nuncio in Havana.

Father Loredo later returned to teaching in the archdiocesan seminary and was assigned to care for religious and lay communities in some churches attached to religious houses in the city of Havana. In 1985, some years after the period of his sentence was over, Father Loredo chose to leave the country for good, and live elsewhere, where he continued to exercise his ministry.

## The "New" San Carlos y San Ambrosio Seminary

During the 1940s Cardinal Arteaga built El Buen Pastor Archdiocesan Seminary so that he could use the magnificent and history-filled building of the San Carlos Seminary as his Cardinal's Palace. El Buen Pastor Seminary was surrounded by farms belonging to private individuals, and by 1965 many of the farms had been nationalized and turned into military facilities. It seemed that being so close to weapons and ammunition depots posed a danger to the seminarians.

In March 1966 the Ministry of the Armed Forces, using the offices of the papal nunciature, asked the church to sell these lands and buildings of El Buen Pastor Seminary so they could be used for military purposes. The Cuban bishops agreed to negotiate the sale after assuring themselves that the intention of the revolutionary government was, in fact, what it said, and was not to deprive the church of the institution it used for the training of new priests. A mixed commission was set up, and two lay people appointed by the hierarchy represented the church. This commission set the price in line with the legally recognized value of the real estate, which was of course much less than it had been in the earlier days of capitalist society. There was also an agreement that the Ministry of the Armed Forces would provide the church all the materials it might need to repair whatever church property it should choose for reestablishing the seminary, subtracting the cost from the agreed-upon price for the property. The agreement of sale was signed on June 22, 1966.

The archbishop decided to restore the original site of the historic San Carlos y San Ambrosio Seminary, which had been made the Cardinal's Palace but was now not being used, and to reestablish the archdiocesan seminary there.

Under the leadership of the rector, Father Carlos Manuel de Céspedes, and in the new Vatican II spirit and with the old seminary building rehabilitated, the traditional custom of having the seminarians occupy cells was replaced by one in which they lived six or eight to a dormitory. Moreover, discipline became more flexible and seminarians were given greater freedom to determine their own schedule for study, personal meditation, and so forth. The fact that the seminary was located in the downtown area called Old Havana made it possible for the seminarians to spend their free time visiting relatives and friends, going to shows, art exhibitions, and museums. Thus the almost monastic isolation in which seminarians had been educated in the past was swept away. That enabled them to relate to the neighborhood and to everyday Cuban life. Within a few years, as part of their overall training, groups of seminarians voluntarily began to take part in annual work sessions to aid agriculture, like other students in the country. Dropping the use of the cassock was helpful in all of this.

One of the most important changes was the bishops' decision to require that those entering the seminary be graduates of the state high school system, which meant that they had to be at least fifteen years old. Thus the new vocations to the priesthood became more mature and more stable. Similarly, the curriculum updating involved in the new postconciliar guidelines for the liberal arts, philosophy, and theology, and in the requirement that seminarians do practical pastoral work in the parishes of the archdioceses led to a remarkable improvement in the formation of new aspirants to the priesthood in Cuba.

Similar changes were likewise introduced in San Basilio Minor Seminary in the archdiocese of Santiago de Cuba. For several more years, however, that seminary remained in the building that had been built next to the national shrine of the Virgin Mary of Charity, in the town of El Cobre, near Santiago de Cuba. The archbishop of that see some years later decided to transfer the seminary to a more centrally located church property in the city of Santiago.

Finally, it should be pointed out that not all of these positive changes, providentially set in motion by the military needs of the country, were initially well received by all seminarians, priests, and lay people. Despite these changes and others that followed, Cuban seminarians—like the church in general—have not kept pace with rest of the Cuban people.

## Obligatory Military Service

On November 16, 1963, the revolutionary government decreed the law establishing obligatory military service, which meant that male citizens from seventeen to forty-five years of age could not leave the country. This measure, imposed in response to the defense requirements of the country, applied to all, and naturally fell on all Catholics, including the Cuban clergy. Some interpreted this measure as an attempt to deprive them of their freedom and their dignity.

Three young priests were drafted in 1966 and were made members of the Military Units to Aid Production (UMAP), those units to which recruits not considered politically trustworthy tended to be assigned. These priests, who took this unexpected experience well, were allowed to leave before their legal period of three years was over. Subsequently one of them left the country, but another, Alfredo Petit, would later be given high responsibilities in the chancery office in his diocese, and the third one, Jaime Ortega, was raised to the episcopacy.

Significantly, when Bishop Pedro Meurice Estiú, then the auxiliary and later the archbishop of Santiago de Cuba, was called up as a reservist because he fell within the age limit, he was offered all kinds of excuses and an order was given that permitted him to return to his ecclesiastic duties.

Just like countless lay people, some seminarians were drafted when various calls for military service were issued. Most of them returned to study for the priesthood when their terms were over.

## The Reorganization of the Lay Apostolate

After 1962, for practical purposes the movement of the lay apostolate was narrowed down to Catholic Action, since almost all the other organizations were made a part of it, under the guidelines of the Cuban bishops. Catholic Action maintained its original basic structure of four branches divided by age and sex. The former specialized youth movements (JOC, JEC, JUC) were abolished and their functions were incorporated into Catholic Action. The specialized movements had already been reduced to a very small number of young people, who raised suspicions in the minds of the revolutionary authorities, given the political situation, and thus they encountered mistrust and discrimination in school and work. As a result of the consolidation, Catholic Action was enriched with the membership of the Marian congregations, the Dominican, Franciscan, and Carmelite third orders, the Knights of Columbus, the Daughters of Isabel, and several confraternities.

Given these circumstances, and as a way of supporting the smaller numbers of clergy and filling in for them, the lay leadership of Catholic Action agreed to direct their work along four lines: formation (theology courses for lay people), liturgy (carrying out lay ministries in liturgy and paraliturgies), apostolate (personally proselytizing through witness of life), and catechesis (teaching children and preparing adults for the sacraments). Although this decision was approved by the Cuban Bishops Conference, it found little support among the clergy and was even explicitly opposed in some dioceses such as that of Camagüey, which was beginning to experiment with community-oriented pastoral work under the direction of the Belgian priests who were working there and whose more or less open influence was at work in other dioceses, like Cienfuegos.

The result was a contradictory situation: on the one hand, the lay activists in Catholic Action took over ecclesiastical tasks while significantly neglecting their secular commitments and their own specific lay witness; on the other hand, lay leaders were taken more seriously in planning and carrying out pastoral activity. The result was unquestionably a distortion of the life of the church, since missing from the lay contribution was the incarnate secular experience that must characterize it; moreover, laity and clergy often failed to work together.

One indication of how confused things were during this period is the fact that of the four basic activities of Catholic Action at that period, the only one that was not clearly and coherently defined in people's awareness and in practice was that of the apostolate, even though that was the most basic element. Many came to believe that the apostolate was a matter of recruiting lay people to do religious artwork for churches. Others thought it meant "living witness," which was interpreted as a readiness to avoid taking part in the revolution by not participating in social organizations and mass undertakings; part of this "witness" was then that these people would stoically accept the consequences when the time came to measure their level of sacrifice and degree of usefulness to society in workplace or school. Naturally, this notion meant that many Catholics were falling further behind as the masses moved forward.

These developments and the new ideas of community pastoral work deriving from Vatican Council II prompted the bishops and the lay leadership to disband Catholic Action and replace it with a simpler and more community-oriented organization, which was integrated into the church's overall pastoral work. The step was actually taken at Cuban Catholic Action's National Assembly, held in the city of Cienfuegos in August 1967, when it offered to the hierarchy a proposal for an Organized Lay Apostolate (ASO; Apostolado Seglar Organizado). That arrangement was approved for the whole country.

Basically the Organized Lay Apostolate was a matter of bringing lay people into episcopal commissions and into diocesan and parish councils and commissions so that they could work with the hierarchy and clergy in the church's community-oriented pastoral work. This new orientation given to the Lay Apostolate seemed to be a step backward rather than forward toward the recognition of the autonomy of the laity, since the lay people taking part in the ecclesiastical bodies were usually chosen by the hierarchy and clergy from among those people who were most in tune with their criteria and directions. That was true even in what is most properly lay: the social, economic, and political realms. Hence the Cuban church was deprived of the pluralism that is so necessary in periods of social change.

## The Cuban Delegation to the Third Worldwide Congress of the Lay Apostolate

Not since the delegation of bishops who went from Cuba to take part in the sessions of Vatican II was there any delegation from Cuba to another country as broad-based as the one that officially represented the Cuban church in the huge Third Worldwide Congress of the Lay Apostolate, held in October 1967. (During this period some Catholic individuals who had left the country had attended international meetings as members of the Cuban church, even when for practical purposes they had deserted the Cuban church when they left their country. Such incidents led the president of the Cuban Bishops Conference to request the Holy See in the name of the Cuban church not to accept any representation from the dioceses of Cuba unless they had come from Cuban territory and had the authorization of their bishop.)

The delegation was made up of six Cuban lay leaders, and was headed by one of them. Auxiliary Bishop Fernando Azcárate of Havana, who was then president of the Bishops Commission for the Lay Apostolate, served as adviser. The bishops of Pinar del Río and Matanzas did not provide any representatives from their dioceses for the delegation, and the archdiocese of Santiago de Cuba was unable to send its delegate. Attending the congress were delegates of Cuban origin who had left the country and were members of delegations from other countries.

This first encounter between Cuban Catholic laity and the worldwide situation of the church, after so many years of isolation and lack of information, enabled people to discover ways of being Catholic that were different from the traditional and ultraconservative form that was still common in Cuba. Delegates to the congress were able to explain that discovery in detail to diocesan and parish communities in Cuba after they returned. They communicated their findings by means of a series of conferences, meetings, and conversations held throughout the island. This witness enabled some Catholics to free themselves from obsolete ways of living the faith and to find more genuine ways of living it and of putting their love into practice in the social context of their country during this period. Others, however, were unmoved by this situation of church life today.

Subsequent conspiratorial activities by some of these delegates, however, once more hindered the improvement of church-state relations.

## The Appointment of an Auxiliary Bishop for Santiago de Cuba

The large size of the old archdiocese of Santiago de Cuba, the fact that the few available clergy were very spread out, and the age of Archbishop Enrique Pérez Serantes led the Holy See to appoint an auxiliary bishop. Father Pedro Meurice Estiú was chosen. Aged thirty-five, he had had a good deal of experience as a pastor and as a diocesan council member for Catholic Action. Furthermore, he had a relatively clear understanding of the social processes taking place in Cuba.

On August 30, 1967, Father Meurice was ordained a bishop in the national shrine of Our Lady of Charity in the town of El Cobre, near Santiago de Cuba. The local civil authorities gave the church permission to celebrate fully the liturgical ceremonies and subsequent feast days. Hundreds of the faithful took part.

By this time the Cuban Catholic church was beginning to prepare for the Second General Conference of Latin American Bishops, which was to be celebrated the following year in the city of Medellín, Colombia. The church was becoming aware of how mistaken it had been during previous years—and began to search for the most adequate way to carry out its prophetic mission. For practical purposes this closes the phase that we have called one of flight, whether in the form of emigration to other countries or of inhibition and uneasiness on the part of those faced with the signs of the times. A new phase, encompassing the following ten years, a "re-encounter" with the people, now begins to take place.

# 5

# Re-encounter (1968–1978)

In late 1967 the Cuban church began to acquire a new awareness of its mission. Vatican Council II and the new Latin American theology were challenging its traditional ecclesiology. The fact that its own triumphalist strivings for dominance had been defeated and its subsequent flight from its responsibility to evangelize concretely in a particular time and place began to threaten the Cuban church's very survival. The Cuban church began to comprehend that its site in history *is* Cuba, its mission is to serve, and its structure is one of community.

During the new phase ushered in with the Medellín Conference, Vatican II was made specific in a concern for development that led the Cuban church to discover that many of the measures and accomplishments of the Cuban revolution were ethically on the mark. During this phase the hierarchy became completely Cuban, as did most of the clergy, and both were rejuvenated. The direction from the Vatican was one of openness to the social changes taking place in the world. All this led the Cuban bishops to give up their isolation and silence and to make their first concrete demonstrations of solidarity with the Cuban people, who were striving to build a new society, one more just and humane, despite so many obstacles.

Although the initial mistrust was not completely overcome, conspiracy became a thing of the past, Catholics were no longer encouraged to leave the country, and in practice the church authorities began to re-enter into contact with the authorities and with the people.

## The Second General Conference of Latin American Bishops (Medellín, Colombia, 1968)

The Medellín Conference was a great leap forward for the Catholic church in Latin America. In this predominantly Catholic continent, the church still held onto the most triumphalist characteristics of Christendom. The beginnings of the imperialist strategy of "national security" in Brazil offered the Catholic church the chance to present itself to the people as an alternative to socialist revolution. At their meeting the bishops took into account the experience of Brazilian Christian base communities. The conclusions of the conference exhibited an explicit condemnation of classic capitalism and an advocacy of reformist developmentalism that was entirely new to Latin American Catholicism.

In Cuba there was a good deal of preparation for Medellín as the bishops, clergy, and lay leadership belonging to pastoral commissions and councils studied the preparatory documents. This discussion was the most beneficial aspect of the opening of the Cuban Catholic community to what was happening elsewhere. A delegation of five bishops from Cuba attended the conference. Accompanying the delegation as an expert in sociology was Father Francisco Oves Fernández, still just a priest, who had returned to Cuba in 1965 and already stood out for his progressive positions.

The closed-in structure of the Cuban church made it impossible for its grass roots to be organized into small communities of like-minded people experiencing the overall thrust of events in society. Those who exposed themselves to ongoing history, and who, impelled by their faith, were increasingly involved in the revolutionary activity of the people, soon encountered mistrust and rejection from many members of the Catholic community. Nevertheless, the hierarchy began to dialogue with the political authorities of the country from time to time. This was not the formal kind of dialogue some bishops desired, for conditions were not ready yet. It was, rather, a series of direct contacts between representatives of the bishops and the governmental authorities, whenever circumstances required it, and not only through the good offices of the nunciature, as had been the case up to this point. This new attitude enabled the younger sectors of clergy and laity to show that they understood that lay people must become involved in the country's new social structures.

This was the most important impact on Cuba of the Medellín Conference, since one could not yet speak of a theological renewal in the Cuban church.

## The Death of Archbishop Enrique Pérez Serantes

Old and prevented from getting around his diocese by failing health, Archbishop Enrique Pérez Serantes died in Santiago de Cuba on April 18, 1968. His popularity and the contradictions he embodied were reflected in the way people reacted at his death. The faithful of Cuba, and especially of Santiago and Camagüey, recalled the way he had untiringly made the rounds of the most remote places in his dioceses in a most humble and simple fashion during the many years he served them as bishop. Nor did the Cuban people or the top leadership of the revolution forget the way he bravely stood up to the authorities of the deposed tyranny, demanding assurances that Fidel Castro and those who attacked the Moncada barracks with him in 1953 would be given a fair trial. Nor did anyone forget his pastoral letters against communism, although each gave his or her own interpretation. Those letters came from an understandable ideological fear that went along with his age, training, and situation, but they were also motivated by a sincere love for the people of Cuba.

Hence there was nothing surprising about the fact that the first floral arrangements to arrive at the cathedral in Santiago de Cuba at the time of the funeral were those of Fidel Castro and his brother Raúl, with whom Pérez Serantes always maintained excellent personal relations; nor was the huge popular outpouring during the funeral any surprise. The archbishop's funeral rites were celebrated in solemn fashion in the cathedral that had been his see during the last twenty years of his life. All the Cuban bishops were there, as were representatives of the diplomatic corps and the revolutionary government. Leading figures of the Catholic laity, both local and national, were also among the crowd that overflowed the church.

The funeral march passed through the city from the cathedral to the Santa Efigenia Cemetery, with a long procession of the faithful on foot. The city authorities did all they could to aid the funeral. Although it took place during working hours and there had been no resolution suspending work, the whole city of Santiago de Cuba practically came to a halt as people went out onto the streets, balconies, and rooftops while the funeral procession passed by. It was a genuine showing of great respect.

After Archbishop Pérez Serantes's death, Auxiliary Bishop Pedro Meurice Estiú administered the archdiocese temporarily until he was made archbishop. From that moment onward, the Cuban episcopate has been made up entirely of Cubans.

## Visits from Archbishop Pironio and Other Important Figures

On September 8, 1969, Archbishop Eduardo F. Pironio visited Cuba in connection with his election as president of the Latin American Bishops Council (CELAM). Archbishop Pironio made another visit to Cuba in mid-January 1970. During these visits he met with members of the hierarchy, the clergy, and lay leaders, and also with government officials. These visits indicated that the universal church was beginning to show interest in the Cuban church. Previously the only visits made had been those of well-known lower-level church figures such as the Belgian sociologist Father François Houtart, the Argentine sociologist Father Aldo Büntig, Bishop Eugenio de Araujuo Sales of the Department of Social Action in CELAM, and Father Michel Quoist, the French writer, among others.

However, after Archbishop Pironio's visit there were visits from Father Pedro Arrupe, the head of the Jesuits; Bishop (now Cardinal) Agostino Casaroli; Archbishop Antonio Quarracino, the president of the Department of the Laity in CELAM; Archbishop Maximino Romero de Lema, secretary of the Sacred Congregation for the Clergy; Bishop Alfonso López Trujillo, general secretary of CELAM; Cardinal Bernadine Gantin, president of the Pontifical Commission for Justice and Peace; as well as others. Some of these figures came into contact with the Catholic communities of Cuba through liturgical concelebrations, informal conversations, and interviews, and could thus exchange impressions with the various sectors of Cuban Catholicism, and sometimes with the state and the party.

Both the government and church press gave prominent coverage to the meetings some of these visitors had with Fidel Castro, particularly Cardinals Casaroli and Gantin, Bishop Manuel Viera Pinto of Mampula, Mozambique, and Bishop Sergio Méndez Arceo of Cuernavaca, Mexico, who subsequently visited Cuba many times, offering genuine and honest "accompaniment" to the Cuban people.

It was also during this stage of the history of the Cuban church that the Department of Vocations and Ministries of CELAM held its regional meeting for Central America and the Caribbean in Santiago de Cuba. The bishops and priests of that department visited several parts of the island and came into contact with various Catholic communities in which they also concelebrated the Eucharist. Some of their visits to historic sites were sponsored by the Cuban Institute of Friendship with Peoples (ICAP). Some of these visiting bishops made statements to Cuban and foreign news agencies, expressing their admiration for the way the Cuban Catholic church and its communities were developing.

## The Economic Blockade of Cuba by the United States

On April 20, 1969, the Cuban bishops signed a statement addressed to all priests and all the faithful, in which they said:

> Seeking the welfare of our people and the faithful, in the service of the poorest in accordance with Christ's command, and in the commitment proclaimed once again in Medellín, we denounce this unjust situation of blockade, which adds to unnecessary suffering and makes development efforts more difficult. Therefore we appeal to the conscience of those who are in a position to resolve it to undertake decisive and effective actions aimed at bringing about an end to this measure.

The church was explicitly condemning the immoral economic blockade that the American government had imposed on the people of Cuba.

At the request of the bishops, Father Francisco Oves, who was then the president of the Commission for Pastoral Work, played a large role in drafting this document. It took four drafts to bring about unanimity among the bishops. The condemnation at the end of the document was a surprise simply because no one expected it and because it was unanimous on the part of the bishops, which discouraged any theoretical rationale for the event that might have been offered. The document was the first sign that the previous line of the bishops, as expressed in their 1959 Circular Letter, was being corrected—a result of the new evangelical viewpoint then emerging under the impact of Vatican Council II and the Medellín Conference of CELAM.

The bishops ordered that the letter be read the following Sunday in all Masses celebrated in Cuba. Nevertheless, there were priests who refused to read it, and many of the faithful, whose ideological positions were being challenged, criticized this statement by the bishops. At the same time, other sectors in the church felt supported and stimulated by this new direction taken by the bishops. The new kinds of contradictions emerging in the church, which prompted the statement, were the first sign of vitality shown in the church.[1]

## The Elevation of Father Oves to the Episcopacy

Father Francisco Oves Fernández had returned to Cuba in 1965 after graduate study in sociology at the University of Comillas and in Rome. At first he went to work in his own diocese of Camagüey, but he was soon appointed president of the Bishops Commission on Pastoral Work and professor at San Carlos y San Ambrosio Seminary; hence he moved to Havana.

Due to failing health, Bishop Alfredo Müller San Martín of Cienfuegos needed an auxiliary bishop. Father Oves was appointed to that position and on July 16, 1969, the feast of the Virgin Mary of Carmel, he was ordained a bishop in the cathedral of the diocese of Cienfuegos.

Delegations from all the dioceses of Cuba and from a number of religious orders in the country went to Cienfuegos for Oves's ordination as bishop. Bishop Müller was a gracious host, and government authorities, both local and national, were helpful to him on that occasion.

### The Cuban Bishops' Statement on Faith and Atheism

Along the same lines of realistic renewal that had led them to condemn the blockade, the Cuban bishops issued a new communiqué to the priests and faithful of the land, on September 8, 1969, the feast of Our Lady of Charity, patroness of Cuba. In that statement they analyzed the troublesome question of faith and atheism.

The document refers to "the concrete conditions in which the Cuban catechumen must live the good news of our salvation in Christ," and to the "witness of Christ in these concrete conditions of our national community, which are unprecedented in Latin America." Along this line of concrete theological and pastoral realism the bishops offer guidance to Catholics:

> We must approach the atheist with all the respect and family-spirited charity that one deserves simply by being a human being. We should not rule out the possibility that such a person has come to that position honestly, for it may be very sincere; nor should we avoid working with the person in the practical realm of our earthly endeavors. For example, in development efforts, and in the advancement of all people and of the whole person, there is a vast field for the common endeavor of all people of good will, whether they be atheists or believers.

In this same spirit, the bishops recommend to Catholics

> that they know how to be calmly objective in accepting those healthy elements in the critique of religion that can serve to purify the faith, and that they reflect seriously and prepare themselves so as to know how to distinguish these healthy elements from destructive and false criticism.

This new pastoral attitude on the part of the Cuban bishops set the tone for this most recent stage in the history of the Cuban church, marking the beginning of the gradual acceptance of the involvement of members of the Cuban Catholic community in the labor, student, administrative, social, and mass organizations created by the revolution. This process began with younger lay people and with a greater understanding of the revolutionary social process by the church as a whole.

A number of events within the Latin American Catholic church, which began to reveal new ways of living out the faith and political commitment of Christians, resonated in some sectors of the Cuban church, especially among the young who were growing up in this new atmosphere. The effect began to be felt in pastoral thinking. Among these developments were the death in combat of the Colombian priest and sociologist, Camilo Torres, and the publication, by the University of Havana, of a collection of his studies and other documents; the frequent presence in Cuba of those persecuted for political reasons; and visits from priests, and even some bishops, with progressive theological positions. Many were not exactly political activists but simply sincere people of faith whose vision opened out to other perspectives that the Cuban church had not yet taken into consideration.

Moreover, new worldwide currents of theology had also begun to come to Cuba despite the blockade, particularly those connected with the fate of Latin America. These new currents encouraged people to tackle issues connected with the economic and social emancipation of the peoples of the continent.

## The National Conference of the Lay Apostolate (1969)

After the disbanding of Cuban Catholic Action, the Bishops Conference for the Lay Apostolate, headed by Auxiliary Bishop Fernando Ascárate of Havana, organized a national meeting of lay church leaders from all dioceses. This conference took place in La Milagrosa Convent of the Daughters of Charity in Havana, on August 16–17, 1969, which was less than a month before the bishops' statement on faith and atheism was issued. The fact that Archbishop Zacchi, the chargé d'affaires for the

Holy See in Cuba, was present at the closing ceremony, when the conclusions from the discussion groups were read and approved, served to emphasize the importance of this event. Throughout the entire meeting, Bishop Francisco Oves, then the auxiliary bishop of Cienfuegos, played a highly visible role.

Among the conclusions reached by broad consensus were the following:

> It was observed that the magisterium of the church views the integral development of humans and of human societies as the path to fullness in Christ and the reason why Christians should be positively and actively involved in human strivings for development. Consequently, it was clear that for Christians such participation is not optional, but a duty in conscience.
>
> It was concluded that this call of Christ and his church involves our presence and participation in the efforts for development being carried out today in Cuba, which means that in general we Christians should remain in our country. . . .
>
> Participants thought that with regard to the problems of a developing society it is not enough that Christians as individuals take a stand but that what is needed is a community stance on the part of the church encompassing pastors and laity in a single commitment.

Among the more noteworthy recommendations that the participants proposed to the bishops and asked to be communicated to local communities are the following:

> That our witness of love and service not be limited to words and intellectual studies, but that it be authenticated by consistent deeds, acts, and behavior.
>
> That the hierarchy be encouraged in some explicit fashion to help Christians understand better the reasons why they should remain in our country and take part in collective efforts for development and that the bishops also exhort people to assume personally this posture of remaining and becoming involved where we are.

Finally, one recommendation made as a result of statements by Archbishop Zacchi to the conference—a recommendation that Bishop Azcárate vigorously defended at the closing session, but which was eliminated from the written report at the subsequent request of several delegates and some priests—read as follows:

> That there be an effort to assure that the prominent positions or responsibilities in the church (lay apostolate; liturgy—those who lead prayer, read the Scripture, or bring the offerings; and catechesis) be occupied and carried out by Christians with a positive attitude who have chosen to remain in the country, since that will give witness that the church will remain in Cuba; . . . this, however, should not prevent those Christians who for justifiable personal reasons decide to leave the country from participating fully and helping insofar as they can. In this effort the motives of community charity (even toward them) prompting this decision should be explained with sensitivity to those Christians who decide to leave.[2]

The general effects of this new stance declared at that moment by the church's lay leaders provoked serious controversy. The impact was soon felt in the pastoral line that was to be taken during this phase, whose distinguishing characteristic was practical dialogue.

## An Ecumenical Opening

The opening to the Christian ecumenical movement that Vatican Council II began in the universal Catholic church did not take effect immediately. The Cuban bishops did not decide to permit Catholics to take part officially in ecumenical activities in the country—in connection with other Christian churches and with the Council of Evangelical Churches of Cuba—until they received the Directory prepared by the Secretariat for Christian Unity and approved on April 28, 1967, by His Holiness Paul VI, in order to carry out "what Vatican Council II recommended with regard to ecumenism."

Working out pastoral guidelines in this matter was the task of the Cuban Bishops Commission for Ecumenism, which was set up for that purpose. Initially, Bishop Fernando Azcárate was appointed its head; Father Carlos Manuel de Céspedes also played a very important role. Catholic ecumenism has never amounted to more than overcoming the condemnations of other Christians and their churches, made in history; participating in the Week of Prayer for Christian Unity in which Catholic priests and evangelical pastors join together for prayer and study meetings; exchanging pulpits on special occasions; and allowing certain bishops, priests, and lay people to take part in the activities of evangelical ecumenical organizations. Catholic ecumenism in Cuba did not have an adequate understanding of the relationship with nonbelievers; it has been understood as dialogue with the world, and has been studied only superficially by the Bishops Commission for the Doctrine of the Faith. On the institutional level the Catholic church is not a member of the Council of Evangelical Churches in Cuba. Bishops, priests, and lay people have taken part in its activities but only as individuals.

Perhaps the most significant move in this field was that taken by the Catholic bishops in setting up the Center for Ecumenical Studies (CENDESEC) as a Catholic ecumenical institution. It has made room for Protestant theologians on its advisory board, and brothers and sisters from other Christian denominations have taken part in its activities. The bishops put a Catholic layman in charge of this center. In Protestant circles that was interpreted as proof of the esteem in which lay people were held by the Catholic church. The lack of support for this institute on the part of the Catholic clergy showed that this interpretation was mistaken. After 1971 the lack of support ruined this project. With the resignation of the director in 1972 its institutional activity ceased.

After 1971 the leading Catholic figures drew back from national ecumenical activities to some extent, but at the same time there was a greater participation by lay figures in the activities of the Ecumenical Council of Cuba, in ecumenical events in honor of Camilo Torres, and in the activities of ecumenical movements like the Christian Peace Conference, the

Christian Student Movement, the Latin American Union of Ecumenical Youth, Ecumenical Latin American Social Action, and so forth. All of this took place with the knowledge of the hierarchy and, in some instances, with the personal support of one bishop or another.

## The Resignation of Bishop Díaz Cía and the Appointment of Oves Fernández

On September 29, 1970, His Holiness Paul VI accepted the resignation of Archbishop Evelio Díaz Cía of Havana. Bishop Evelio, as he was usually called in Cuba, suffered from various health problems, including a recently discovered heart ailment. He had already repeatedly told close friends and co-workers that he felt very inadequate in dealing with his responsibilities as a bishop. His failing health undoubtedly contributed to this feeling, but he was also known for his extreme modesty and humility. Hence not until his heart problem appeared did the Holy See accept his resignation. His personal virtues, patriotism, and love for the people gave him the inspiration to discern problems and come to decisions in situations, from 1959 onward, whose newness and complexity went beyond his personal experiences and those of the church itself. After his resignation he was made archbishop emeritus of Havana.

The freedom of action and trust that Archbishop Díaz Cía always granted his co-workers gave the church in Havana an extraordinary atmosphere of freedom and creativity, whose only obstacle was the lack of confidence and lack of understanding among those very co-workers.

After accepting Archbishop Evelio's resignation and after hearing opinions from many people, the Holy See decided to seek a long-term solution for the archdiocese by appointing the young priest Francisco Oves Fernández to succeed Díaz Cía.[3]

The appointment of Archbishop Oves aroused great expectation in the archdiocese and throughout the Cuban church. The fact that he was young and had a broad cultural background, and especially the prestige he enjoyed as a sociologist, in addition to his courteous manner, led people to believe that the serious problems confronting the church would be resolved in short order. Time would show the naïveté of such an illusion, but it would also give evidence of the new archbishop's clarity of vision and his steadfast character and prudence. It would further show the intrinsic difficulty of the problems that had to be solved and the lack of understanding and unrealistic expectations still present in the church.

On October 26, 1970, Bishop Evelio Ramos Díaz, the former rector of El Buen Pastor and San Carlos y San Ambrosio seminaries, was made auxiliary bishop of Havana. Bishop Ramos died suddenly on November 25, 1976, while on a plane flight to Spain for medical treatment.

## The Resignation of Bishop Müller and the Appointment of Prego

Something similar to the situation in Havana took place in the diocese of Cienfuegos when Bishop Alfredo Müller resigned, also because of failing health. The Holy Father accepted Bishop Müller's resignation on July 29, 1971, and on that same date appointed as his successor Bishop Fernando Prego. Prego had been ordained auxiliary bishop of the diocese on January 14 of that same year, replacing Bishop Francisco Oves, who, as we have just seen, had been given charge of the archdiocese of Havana. Because he was young and outgoing, Bishop Prego's joining the episcopacy signaled a promising rejuvenation for the Cuban Catholic hierarchy.

## The National Congress of Education and Culture

The First National Congress of Education and Culture met in Havana on April 23–30, 1971. Among the many foreign intellectuals invited to take part were the Colombian Catholic sociologist Oscar Maldonado and a number of Latin American and European priests.

At first these visitors had little contact with the Cuban church. The Casa de las Americas invited several of them to have a public discussion, and some seminarians and young Cuban priests attended. Later they mentioned their personal disappointment at what seemed to be the high degree of "politicization" and "scant spirituality" of these foreign priests. That gives some sense of the general attitude of young Cuban priests at that time. Later Maldonado had deep and extensive contact with the Cuban church when he carried out a socioreligious study of it under the sponsorship of the International Federation of Socio-Religious Studies (FERES), headed by the Belgian priest François Houtart.

The congress took up a number of themes, including the position with regard to religion, which was summarized in the conclusions as follows:

> 2. The policy of the revolution toward religion has been based on the following principles:
>
> *a)* Not regarding the phenomenon of religion as the center or most important element of our work. Our fundamental effort must be directed toward building socialist society, naturally with the consequent duty of paying attention to and laying out the steps the revolution must make in ideological struggle.
>
> *b)* Absolute separation of church and state, and church and school in all fields.
>
> *c)* Neither fomenting, supporting, nor aiding any religious group, nor asking anything from them.
>
> *d)* We do not share religious beliefs or worship, nor do we support them.
>
> *e)* The revolution respects religious beliefs and worship as the individual right of each person. It imposes nothing, and does not persecute or repress anyone for his or her religious beliefs.
>
> *f)* Centered on building socialism, the revolution offers everyone space and opportunity in its work for change, regardless of whether he or she professes religious beliefs or not.
>
> *g)* With regard to obscurantist and counterrevolutionary sects, the position is to unmask and combat them.
>
> 3. The instrument for the basic struggle of the revolution was defined as:

> *a)* Scientific education in school to combat lies, fraud, and the counterrevolutionary farce.
>
> *b)* The accomplishments of the revolution: profound changes in the social, economic, and political spheres.
>
> Finally it was noted that since we are materialists and Marxist-Leninists, our path should not be that of crude opposition to religion, but scientific education, the raising of the cultural level of the people, and offering teachers educational materials for that purpose.[4]

These principles summarized the policies followed by the revolution throughout the previous years. They had not always been observed in practice due to the passions aroused during the years of confrontation, just as many Christians failed to validate the gospel with their lives during those years. These principles seemed to be in line with the two most recent statements by the Cuban bishops in 1969, and anticipated the principles that the First Congress of the Cuban Communist party would lay down four years later. The net result was that theoretical foundations were laid down paving the way for the practical dialogue that was to unfold between the church and the revolutionary state.

## Statements by Fidel Castro in Chile

The statements about the church, Christians, and religion made by Fidel Castro during his trip to Chile in November 1971 were especially important in the context of the new relationship that characterized this stage of the history of the Cuban church.

In conversation with students of the University of Concepción, on November 18, Fidel told a questioner:

> We have always been very careful to avoid any kind of persecution or struggle against religion in our country. In fact, the line taken by the revolution with priests involved in counterrevolutionary actions and misdeeds has generally been on the side of generosity. We have preferred to sacrifice the possibility of making an example of them so as not to provide imperialism with the opportunity to present the Cuban Revolution as being against religion.

He added:

> Later on, when the bourgeoisie and the imperialists had nothing more to lose, when they were no longer a social force, when this religious issue and the conflicts that had arisen at the beginning of the revolution were calming down, the churches functioned freely. There is also a school for seminarians in our country and it is training religious. There is peace and harmony despite the efforts that occasionally reappear from outside, from some counterrevolutionary campaign or other, utilizing religious people. It must be said that this peace was achieved, on the one hand, because of the attitude of the revolution, as we have already explained, and because of some religious leaders who were especially concerned and interested in finding ways to come together and resolve the problems that had arisen in our country. So the situation is one of peace and harmony.[5]

In his long interview with a group of Chilean priests, known as "the 200," Fidel commented on the broad field of activity in which Christianity and communism can find common ground.

> Although Christianity may have arisen two thousand years ago as a utopian teaching, like a mere spiritual consolation, I think that in our age it has the possibility of being not a utopian teaching but a real one, and not a spiritual consolation for the suffering human being. It may come about that classes disappear and communist society comes to the fore. How does that contradict Christianity? On the contrary: it will be a re-encountering of Christianity with its early days, in its most just, most human, most moral aspects.[6]

Later on he said:

> I tell you that there is a great deal in common between the aims preached by Christianity and the aims we seek as communists; between the Christian preaching of humility, austerity, the spirit of sacrifice, love for neighbor, and

> everything that goes into the life and behavior of a revolutionary.[7]

Castro's long discourses on these subjects may be summed up in the answer he gave to a student in Concepción: "I tell you unhesitatingly what I think: we must see leftist Christians, revolutionary Christians, as strategic allies in the revolution, not traveling companions. Is that clear?"[8] He reaffirmed that in his dialogue with the students at the State Technical University of Santiago, Chile, several days later when he said, ". . . we said that the alliance was not tactical, that it was not a theory about fellow travelers, but simply a strategic alliance."[9]

Such statements from the leader of the Cuban Revolution could be confusing at first to a communist who might be still ideologically immature, just as they might lead to one-sided interpretations by some ultra-conservative Christians, but they soon found a favorable echo in the behavior of the younger sectors of the Cuban church as well as in subsequent statements by high figures in the Catholic church in Cuba.

## The First Latin American Conference of Christians for Socialism

During Fidel Castro's journey to Chile, the priests with whom he met announced that they were preparing an important continent-level meeting of Christians for Socialism, which was in fact held in April 1972. Some of those priests, while visiting Cuba at the beginning of that year, mentioned it to the Cuban bishops and cordially invited them to represent the Cuban Catholic church at that meeting.

Most of the Cuban bishops and the papal nunciature in Cuba responded warmly to the offer. Through the efforts of Archbishop Francisco Oves of Havana, who was president of the Cuban Bishops Conference, Bishop José M. Domínguez of Matanzas, the conference secretary, and Auxiliary Bishop Evelio Ramos of Havana, and with the approval of Archbishop Cesare Zacchi, the chargé d'affaires of the Holy See, a group of priests, seminarians, and lay Catholics, along with other Cuban Christians, were able to join the delegation from other churches of

Cuba and take part in the conference in Chile. This delegation, which was representative of the most politically progressive sectors of the Christian churches in Cuba, was received warmly both by Chileans themselves and by other delegations. Upon returning to Cuba the group held many meetings with the Christian communities in the country, and that helped to broaden the framework of news and ideological awareness of many Cuban Christians. Subsequently the delegation was able to publish a book documenting the conference, which gathered together all the national news and the main speeches and statements at the event. This material was preceded by a critical study.[10]

## The Bicentennial of San Carlos y San Ambrosio Seminary

A historian has written, "The seminary [of Havana] began to function in 1773 and was for many years the educational institution that contributed the most to Cuba. It left a brilliant record in the history of Cuban culture, and was of a higher quality than the university well into the nineteenth century."[11]

The bicentennial celebration of this church institution, which very early helped to forge Cuban national identity, was highlighted in Cuban cultural circles in 1973 by state agencies. Interesting evidence of the new attitude of the Catholic church in Cuba was the fact that the seminary itself organized a full program to celebrate the anniversary. In addition to the liturgical ceremonies, there was a series of public lectures in which a number of outstanding representatives of Cuban culture were invited to participate. That series demonstrated not only the value the institution has had for the church, but its importance in the birth of Cuban culture, national identity, and patriotism.

By the end of the nineteenth century the seminary had been reduced to training priests, and the University of Havana had replaced it in cultural and political terms. During the period of the bourgeois republic and the socialist revolution, it was simply an educational institution marginal to intellectual life and patriotic activity. Indeed, in more than one respect it was alien to basic popular interests if not hostile to them.

The fact that the seminary celebrated its bicentennial as an event in the history of the Cuban people and not simply of the Catholic church was largely made possible by changes in the church and in the seminary itself during this most recent period. Under the rectorship of Father Carlos Manuel de Céspedes—great-great-grandson of the founder of our country, who bore the very same name[12]—the seminary reassumed the name it had during its most brilliant period, occupied once more its magnificent and historical original buildings, freed its discipline from outdated requirements, broadened its field of study, updated its programs, raised the educational and age requirements for admission, and at the same time began the process of integrating the seminarians into the issues facing ordinary Cuban young people.

At the end of the 1969–70 school year, the rector, Father Céspedes, was chosen to head the Office of the Permanent Committee of the Cuban Bishops Conference and to be pastor of the church of Jesús del Monte in Havana, and thus was replaced as rector of the seminary starting in the 1970–71 academic year. During this period, Archbishop Francisco Oves of Havana took up an idea that Father Céspedes had put in motion in 1968, with the support of Archbishop Evelio Díaz of Havana and of the papal nunciature. In coordination with the country's political authorities, seminarians were able to spend one month a year in productive work in agriculture or construction as part of their course of study and formation, just like other Cuban students. Despite the lack of understanding and the controversy that this decision by the hierarchy encountered in the church, the measure helped many of those who were to be Cuba's new priests to become more socially conscious.

Within this postconciliar spirit, which locally could be called the bicentennial spirit, since it was moving toward becoming part of the present context of life in Cuba, the San Carlos y San Ambrosio Seminary in Havana was headed by the young priest from Camagüey, Father José Luis Rodríguez, who replaced Father Froylán during the 1972–73 year; and by Father José M. Miyares, S. J., during 1973–77. Since then the rectors have been young priests who have graduated from that seminary, such as Fathers Norberto López, Alfredo Petit, and most recently, José

Féliz Pérez. The last-named was a worker-priest who, even though he had to give up his factory work, was able to share with his students his broad experience of being thoroughly involved with the people and their social organizations.

## A Letter from Cuban Catholics to the 1974 Synod

A representative of the Cuban church has always been present at the bishops synods that were initiated by Pope Paul VI in 1967 and held in Rome periodically during his pontificate.

Attending the October 1974 Synod was Archbishop Francisco Oves Fernández of Havana, who was then president of the Cuban Bishops Conference. The topic for study and reflection of this representative meeting of the bishops with the Holy Father was evangelization in today's world. Because of the fundamental importance of this topic, a small group of Cuban lay Catholics, who had carried responsibilities and done work in the church for years, were impelled to address the "venerable Synod fathers," "seeking valid and clear guidance with regard to situations in which our faith, love, and hope are dramatically committed and in conflict."

These Catholics explained that they had discovered that "the sincere witness of our faith has been accepted, though not shared, by other companions in struggle and work who are Marxist and atheist activists, just as we have found that our faith is validly in harmony with, and is clarified by, the sociological analysis and the methodology for action that they contribute to us."

They later said:

> We are seriously disturbed by the ambiguity, whether conscious or unconscious, of our hierarchy, clergy, and ecclesiastical agencies . . . that leads our colleagues in work and struggle, inexplicably but regrettably, not fully to trust our own attitude and Christian witness. Thus any evangelizing value there might be in our aspiration to live in harmony with the good news of Christ is nullified.

In their critique they stated that

abstraction-filled preaching, false impartiality and apoliticism, the lack of love and efficacious solidarity with the exploited, who have been victorious in Cuba but are still oppressed in our Latin American subcontinent and other regions of the world, . . . are a counterwitness that weighs heavily on our consciences and offends our communion with the church. . . . Due to the weight of the Catholic church in our subcontinent, we Cuban—and therefore Latin American—Christians are even more concerned about the activities undertaken, publicly even, by groups in our church . . . at the service—unconsciously, we presume—of the centers of exploitation that still continue to oppress our fellow peoples. . . . We have been horrified to see how traditional pieties are used in those countries, . . . how they have even gone so far as to parade the banners of Hidalgo and of Morelos as Catholic, when in their own time they were repudiated because of the church's own failure to understand. We would be scandalized if long after the fact some should seek to wave the banner of Father Camilo Torres after having failed to understand him at the time of his sacrifice. We would not want to see the painful story of Juana de Lorena repeated on our continent.

Archbishop Oves was kind enough to take this document[13] to the synod. Even though the synod did not respond directly, it did have the chance to hear these concerns expressed. The reflections of the synod prompted Pope Paul VI's Apostolic Exhortation *Evangelii Nuntiandi* and the pastoral letter on evangelization published by the Cuban bishops in an effort to apply the universal teaching in the papal encyclical to the specific conditions of Cuba.

However, the letter these Catholics sent to the synod made the more traditional and reactionary sectors of the church all the more suspicious of its authors.

## The End of Archbishop Zacchi's Diplomatic Term

Monsignor [Cesare] Zacchi was the Holy See's diplomatic representative to the Cuban revolutionary government, starting in 1962 when Bishop Luis Centoz departed and became vice camerlengo in the Holy Roman See. Until December 1967, when he was ordained titular Archbishop of Zella, Monsignor Zacchi was not a bishop of the church. That led to great difficulty in his efforts with the Cuban bishops. In a political context that was already ticklish and thorny, his job was made more difficult by the fact that he was not a nuncio, like Bishop Centoz, but simply an interim chargé d'affaires for the Holy See in Cuba. These limitations stood in sharp contrast to the fact that the Cuban government's accredited representative in the Vatican was Dr. Luis Amado Blanco as plenipotentiary ambassador and head of the Cuban mission.

Archbishop Zacchi's ordination to the episcopacy was therefore highly significant. It was interpreted as a public sign of approval of the diplomatic efforts he had made in Cuba, which had been so attacked by ultra-conservative sectors of the church both in the country and among those who had emigrated. Furthermore, many interpreted his decision to be ordained in Cuba by Archbishop Clarizio, the apostolic delegate in Canada, as a gesture to express his sympathy and love for the Cuban people. For Clarizio had had the same position—that of apostolic delegate—in the Dominican Republic during the 1965 revolution to defend the constitution, a revolution that had been stamped out by United States military intervention. Fidel Castro attended the reception for Archbishop Zacchi after the liturgy of episcopal ordination, thus giving the Cuban bishops the chance to converse frankly and cordially with him for the first time since the revolutionary victory. That event was given wide coverage in the Cuban and international press and prompted widely divergent comments.

Archbishop Zacchi's positive but controversial diplomatic efforts in Cuba were the subject of many cricitisms and false attacks sent to the Holy See by members of the clergy both in Cuba and elsewhere. That led him to offer his resignation to the Holy Father many times, but he was always reaffirmed in his post. Significantly, soon after the death in Rome of the Cuban ambassador, Dr. Luis Amado Blanco, who for several years had been dean of the diplomatic corps recognized by the Holy See, Pope Paul raised Zacchi's rank, making him his nuncio in Cuba.

The revolutionary government did not recognize the validity of the old Treaty of Vienna, which had been signed in the nineteenth century by the colonialist Spanish government then controlling Cuba. In that treaty the signatory countries granted to papal nuncios the right to function as deans of the diplomatic corps independently of the amount of time they might have served in that mission. An exception was made in the case of Archbishop Zacchi and he was recognized as dean during the short month he still remained in Cuba as papal nuncio.

After a long and fruitful diplomatic mission in Cuba, on June 7, 1975, Archbishop Cesare Zacchi was made rector of the Vatican's Pontifical Ecclesiastical Academy (a training school for diplomats). Archbishop Mario Tagliaferri took his place in Cuba.

## The First Congress of the Cuban Communist Party

In December 1975 the Communist party of Cuba held its first congress since coming to power. This secular event, which was of great importance in the history of the Cuban people, by that very fact also had an unquestionable influence on the development of the Catholic church in Cuba. This importance was highlighted by the fact that in the *Programmatic Platform* that it approved, the congress devoted several paragraphs to defining the party's attitude toward religion, and the entirety of one of its theses and resolutions to explaining it.

In its *Programmatic Platform,* the Cuban Communist party states that "among the forms of social consciousness is religion, whose nature it is to be a distorted and fantastic reflection of external reality."[14] In its relationships with different religions and their believers, the party maintains the principles of freedom of conscience, that is:

> the right of citizens to profess a religion or none at all; to practice religious worship as long as they abide by the law; the unacceptability of the utilization of any religion to combat the revolution and socialism; the obligatory nature of the observance of laws and the recognition of the same social rights and responsibilities for believers and nonbe-

> lievers alike; scientific education and lay schooling; aid for the material problems of religious buildings that may require the participation of state agencies.[15]

With regard to its attitude toward religion as ideology, as a form of social consciousness, the party's policy

> is superseded by the battle to build the new society and to consolidate socialist relations of productions. These are its basic points: the systematic and patient communication of the ideas of scientific socialism among the masses; not organizing antireligious campaigns or using coercive means of administrative actions against religion; the rejection of any attempt to isolate believers by attracting them to the concrete tasks of the revolution; the requirement that activists in the party and in the Union of Young Communists receive an ideological formation in accordance with the basic elements of Marxist theory.[16]

In this first congress, the Cuban Communist party was not content simply to ratify the classic principles of Marxist-Leninism with regard to religion. Making use of the method of Marxist analysis in an orthodox manner, it acknowledged and expressed appreciation for the new political manifestations of the religious phenomenon in Latin America and with regard to Cuba. In its first *Programmatic Platform* the congress states: "On the international level and especially in Latin America the party has a positive regard for the activity of many progressive and updated Christian sectors that are participating in struggles for national liberation, confronting imperialism and the local oligarchies, and also making known the accomplishments of the new way of life in Cuba and its socialist revolution as examples to follow."[17] The fact that the Cuban party had objectively recognized this new way of living out Christian faith in real terms did not change the communists' classic conception of religion, but it did broaden the understanding of social reality in that conception and it would enrich its political vision to the extent that the phenomenon was to become more pronounced and develop further.

In the party's thesis on the policy to follow toward religion, the church, and believers, the basis of the *Platform* is made more explicit with a detailed analysis of the various forms that the phenomenon of religion assumes in Cuba. There is an explanation from the traditional Marxist viewpoint of the relationship between the revolution and the Catholic church in recent years, alongside other such relationships, and there is guidance for how these relationships should develop in the years to come. In its resolution on this point, the congress approved the basic lines of the focus developed in the *Thesis.*

In conjunction with this realistic and objective opening relative to these new political expressions of contemporary Christianity, the Cuban Communist party defined an aspect that is important today. The *Thesis* states absolutely that "science and religion are irreconcilably opposed,"[18] a point on which the party is utterly in agreement with the opinion of some "traditionalist" Catholics. If, on the one hand, it states that "believers and nonbelievers are allowed to join mass organizations with equal rights," and "similarly, when candidates are nominated for the organizations of People's Power, they are not required to make any declaration about any religious affiliation or lack of it," the congress immediately goes on to say that "the party and the Union of Young Communists reserve the right to demand that those who enter their ranks have a political and ideological formation fully in accordance with the dialectical materialist theoretical bases on which their program and doctrine are grounded," and that "therefore, the party and the Union of Young Communists . . . do not grant membership to those who do not fully and unreservedly share their Marxist-Leninist doctrine and their scientific and materialistic ideology."[19]

Although the *Resolution* of the full assembly of the congress included only the first part of this last statement, it was to be effective in helping Cuban Christians free themselves from the occasional opportunistic or dishonest temptation to seek to join the Communist party now that it held power in Cuba as the vanguard of the working people. In principle, that did not imply any negative discrimination or any kind of marginalization that would prevent people from participating fully in the activity of the state and of the entire population.[20]

## The Socialist Constitution (1976)

One immediate effect of the First Congress of the Cuban Communist Party was the promulgation of the new constitution of the republic. The draft, prepared by a mixed commission from the party and the government, was enriched with many changes suggested by the people in the broad grassroots discussion it underwent. After being polished in this manner, it was approved by the First Party Congress on February 15, 1976, and then by 99 percent of all Cubans, aged sixteen or older, in a national referendum. Until that date, the Fundamental Law passed by the cabinet of the revolutionary government on February 7, 1959, was in effect, although it had often been modified. That law was a version of the 1940 constitution adapted to the transitional state organization of the revolutionary Cuban state. According to this Fundamental Law:

> *Article 35.* There is free profession of any religion, and free exercise of any worship with no other limitation except respect for Christian morality and public order. The church is to be separate from the state, which will not provide support for any kind of worship.

Elsewhere it says:

> *Article 20.* All Cubans are equal before the law. The republic does not recognize any exemptions or privileges.
>
> Any kind of discrimination for reasons of sex, race, color, class, or any other against human dignity is declared illegal and punishable.
>
> The law will determine the sanctions to be incurred by those who break this precept.

The new 1976 socialist constitution adjusts these basic principles, and safeguards them in accordance with the new situation in society deriving from the revolution. The equality of citizens and religious freedom are laid down in the following fashion:

*Article 40.* All citizens enjoy equal rights and are subject to equal duties.

*Article 41.* Discrimination for reasons of race, color, sex, or national origin is proscribed and is punished by law.

State institutions educate all from their earliest years in the principle of the equality of all human beings.

*Article 54.* The socialist state, which bases its activity on the scientific materialist conception of the universe and teaches that conception to the people, recognizes and guarantees freedom of conscience, the right of each person to profess any religious belief whatsoever and to engage in the worship he or she chooses within respect for the law.

The law regulates the activities of religious institutions.

It is illegal and punishable to set up faith or religious belief in opposition to the revolution, education, or the fulfillment of the duties of working, defending the country with arms, revering its symbols, and other duties established by the Constitution.

The preservation of the principle of socialist legality, the constitutional guarantees given to freedom of conscience and religious worship, and the fact that all citizens were declared equal in rights and duties enabled the church and believers to feel more secure in living out their faith and showing love for neighbor—especially because of the importance people in the country gave to observing the new legislation, which embodied the accomplishments of the revolution. In actuality, the prohibitions contained in the last paragraph of article 54 of the socialist constitution, which were intended to deal with the social behavior of certain pseudo-Christian sects existing in the country, did not prevent the Catholic church or any of the other churches and Christian believers in Cuba from responsibly carrying out their religious activities.

## Condemnation of Terrorism

In late 1976 the Permanent Committee of the Bishops Conference of Cuba released a statement[21] condemning terrorism in general and particularly the destruction of a civilian plane of the

Cuban airlines (Empresa Cubana de Aviación) earlier that year (on October 6) as it was taking off from Barbados, killing all the passengers and crew.[22] This event also prompted Pope Paul VI to send condolences to the Cuban Catholic church.[23]

With this statement, similar to those made by other Christian churches, organizations, and ecumenical movements in Cuba, the Cuban church joined in the denunciations issued by the political, social, and mass organizations of the country and in the sorrow of the whole Cuban people. Fifteen years previously the church might not have felt such solidarity with the feelings of the people, as indicated by its silence over the Bay of Pigs invasion and numerous other terrorist attacks and acts of aggression.

In their statement condemning terrorism, the members of the Permanent Committee of the Cuban Bishops Conference supported the actions taken in this respect by the Cuban prime minister, Fidel Castro, and by the president of Venezuela in response to the criminal action against the airplane, and they singled out "the contribution for human progress represented by the agreements reached at the Helsinki Conference on peaceful coexistence between states."

A significant indicator of this new mutual relationship of solidarity and communication on the part of the Catholic church toward the Cuban people was the fact that when Archbishop Francisco Oves of Havana showed up, anonymously, at the funeral celebration for the victims of this crime, he was recognized and treated with great respect both by the large numbers of people present and by the authorities. They took him from his modest place in the long line of people filing up and brought him straight to the caskets. There the bishop prayed in public, silently, as all around stood quietly in remembrance.

## Statements by Fidel Castro in Jamaica

On October 20, 1977, the president of the State Council and of the Council of Ministers of Cuba, Fidel Castro, met for a long time with representatives of Christian churches in Jamaica during his visit to that neighboring country.

During that conversation, Fidel Castro graphically gave his interpretation of the peculiar characteristics of religion in Cuba, particularly Catholicism. He spoke not only as the country's ruler but also from his experience growing up in a believing family and as a former student in Jesuit schools. He reiterated many of the principles that have guided the socialist revolution in Cuba in its relationships with the churches and with believers. It was clear that the revolution's ideas in this regard have remained firm despite the changing circumstances it has had to confront:

> Throughout history there have been conflicts between revolutions and the church, but I believe these conflicts have been held down to a minimum in Cuba. Indeed there have been such conflicts in our country, but we had these principles and these ideas. One measure we had to take, perhaps the strongest, was that of asking Spanish priests to go back to Spain. However, no church was ever closed, and no one was persecuted for his or her religious ideas. . . . In fact, there were priests involved in conspiracy. . . . We never subjected any priest to any severe sanction, no priest has ever been physically mistreated in our country, no priest and no other citizen. . . . We have harsh laws, in fact, we even have the death penalty for certain crimes; but none of these sanctions was ever applied to a priest. . . . Here's something else: when we felt forced to imprison some priests for very serious counterrevolutionary crimes, they were always released after a short time. We did that on purpose. . . . That was the attitude of the government during the initial conflict period. Things began to improve somewhat, they gradually improved and another spirit developed in the leadership of the Catholic church. . . . I can assure you that no revolutionary process as radical and as deep as the Cuban Revolution has had fewer conflicts with religion than the Cuban Revolution. Today the climate of relations is normal.

With regard to potential collaboration between Christians and Marxists, Castro said:

> It isn't enough to respect each other; we must cooperate with each other in order to change the world. . . . I maintain that the basis for this cooperation must be established before the revolution takes place. . . . I told the Chileans that we should make an alliance, but not a tactical alliance. I was asked whether it was tactical or strategic, and I said a strategic alliance between religion and socialism, between religion and the revolution.

The statements by the president, which repeated all he had previously said on the issue, were much better received in Cuba than those he had made on other occasions.[24]

**The 125th Anniversary of the Death of Father Varela**

On Saturday, February 25, 1978, the 125th anniversary of the death of Father Félix Varela was memorialized in the metropolitan cathedral of Havana. Archbishop Francisco Oves presided over a solemn celebration in which the other bishops of the country, the priests of Havana, students from San Carlos y San Ambrosio Seminary, and many of the faithful participated. The apostolic pronuncio was present and, at the urging of the archbishop of Havana, Archbishop Pedro Meurice Estiú of the see of Santiago de Cuba presented a brilliant exposition on this patriot and priest. This gesture symbolized the unity of the Cuban church, manifest not only in the sacramental sign of the Eucharist, but also for the first time in common tribute offered in memory of this holy Cuban priest, a teacher of Christian virtue and of Cuban identity, Father Félix Varela.

Prior to the service, there were study days devoted to the person and work of Father Varela, held in San Carlos y San Ambrosio Seminary, where he studied and which he later reformed. Never before, not even on the occasion of the 100th anniversary of his birth or of his death, had the Catholic church honored the memory of Father Félix Varela so solemnly and so completely as on this occasion. This was a sign of the new stance that the Cuban Catholic church began to take after almost twenty years of social revolution, and a sign of its incipient aim of becoming incarnate in its people and in its healthiest and most venerable traditions in a way that it had never previously attempted.[25]

## The Eleventh World Festival of Youth and Students

The Eleventh World Festival of Youth and Students was held in Cuba in 1978. Never before had one of these international meetings of young people, which promote friendship, justice, family spirit, and peace among the peoples of the world, been celebrated in the New World.

The festival was an opportunity for many of the 20,000 foreign young people, guests of the Cuban people, to become acquainted with Cuba, its people, its revolution, and even its church. The Catholic church provided Mass in a number of languages in some of the more centrally located churches in Havana, should foreign delegates wish to attend Mass while in Cuba.

Since there were some international Christian organizations on the international organizing committee of the festival, the National Preparatory Committee placed on the program a special meeting between religious delegates and religious figures from the host country. In addition to personal and unofficial contacts, the Catholic church was invited to participate in the Eleventh Festival with an official delegation, which was headed by Archbishop Francisco Oves of Havana, the president of the Bishops Conference of Cuba.

Speaking to the delegates and those invited to the meeting, Archbishop Oves made observations about Christian faith, believers, and social revolution. These statements were perhaps the most serious and most important any Cuban bishop has made on the topic. That fact made him stand out as the most clear-sighted of the bishops at that time. Referring to the existing situation in Cuba Archbishop Oves said:

> To begin with, public-health care is offered free without any discrimination, which is in line with Christian faith, consistent with its demands for a brotherly and sisterly love for all. Second, education is offered to all children, young people, and adults as an opportunity and as a duty. This also fits the aspiration of Christian faith in its concern for

equality and human development. Third, an economy that strives to be motivated not primarily by the yearning for money but by the proven needs of the people is in line with the gospel maxim that one cannot serve God and Money. Fourth, a society that is striving to overcome the antagonism of social classes is more in line with the radical Christian condition.

Actually, at this point we do not think that we are in a period of instability or of groping but, rather, that in our living, the positions concisely, firmly, and clearly set out in article 54 of our socialist constitution are being carried out. We would go so far as to express the hope that in the future there may be further development in the vital relationship between revolution and believer, revolution and church. . . . It is our intention, through our Christian identity, to carry out activities whose direction will be toward promoting a responsible and sincere participation in this, our socialist society.

As practical expressions of such attitudes and without being immodest, I would like to point to the public manifestations that the church has sought to make—I speak in the name of the Catholic church—through its teaching authority. It has said No to the blockade, . . . for in gospel fashion it understands that from the standpoint of international social morality this is a violation of international social justice; it has said Yes to life, the right to life, and hence No to terrorism; it has said Yes to participation, sharing in the responsibilities of building this, our new society.

Naturally, we are quite convinced that problems are part of the risk of our human life. . . . These problems to which I refer, in all kindness and love can be solved, I believe, through article 54 of our socialist constitution. I believe that its application could overcome any kind of discrimination toward believers to the extent that their attitude becomes one of loyalty, competence, honesty, and sincerity, and is inspired by the gospel.

The shape of today's world suggests that there be a rethinking of Christian faith with regard to the exercise of freedom of conscience. Hence we believe that if Christian faith is taken always and exclusively as an ideology, one that is always negative, it will be harder to understand the believer—and all believers—as making up the family of God, which is the church. Furthermore, we judge that there would perhaps be a danger of unintentionally violating that freedom of conscience and there would not be offered an encouraging example of the way our socialist legal framework shows respect and allows full activity. Thus we believe that it would be necessary to keep in mind that Christian faith is not an ideology. However, we must confess with complete honesty and with deep historical, human, and gospel humility that Christian faith has been manipulated ideologically. We have made progress in discerning such manipulation. In that respect Marxist social science has made a contribution.

However, since Christian faith is not an ideology, we would like to suggest, with deep respect and Christian love, the following two formulations. We do this independently of what institutions may determine, since institutions naturally have the right to lay down the conditions people must meet to participate in them. Here is the formulation I was referring to: first, the non-necessity of belief and, second, non-belief not a necessity.

All this, as I see it, is relevant to the evangelizing vision of Christ present in his church, today, here and now, and for all humans. But it is also relevant for envisioning and setting up a new social order in all the other countries of Latin America, Africa, and Asia, where it may be necessary, and even in the capitalist countries themselves. The ideal of a society without conflicting economic or social classes is more in line with the gospel demand for brother- and sister-hood in Christ. However, I ask myself, how can we help one another to make it possible for Christians to be committed to the gradual realization of this ideal, if Christian faith is always presented as something inevitably hostile? I believe I am formulating the sincere desires of many believers and of many Christians around the world when I say that, in expressing the desire for a rethinking of the phenomenon of religious faith in its distinct origins, we

> do not think we are giving in to, or suggesting any kind of, revisionism insofar as that serves the purposes of the imperialist forces. We would like to base this rethinking on the principles of Marxist social science itself, which does not separate theory from reality. On the contrary, we believe this would have a great impact on the commitment of all Christians from all countries, so as to coordinate a common effort with all those who are striving for a new society, free of domination, on both national and international levels. . . .
>
> In this I would like to see—and I invite you to share in it with deep respect—the desire for a mutual attitude befitting an attitude that is honest in human terms, and never opportunistic.[26]

These words gave a new dimension of breadth and depth to the re-encounter that had begun on the part of the church in Cuba just ten years before.

**Dialogue with the Cuban Community Living Abroad**

Another important gesture demonstrating that the Catholic church's pastoral practice was gradually taking on the genuine interests of the Cuban people was the statement made by the Cuban bishops in support of the program proposed by the revolutionary government for dialogue in order to reunify the Cuban family.

The Permament Committee of the Cuban Bishops Conference said, "We want to manifest publicly our pastoral support for this dialogue, due to the proposals made at a propitious moment by our president of the State Council, Fidel Castro. Broad sectors of those who share our nationality and who for different reasons are living outside our country have begun to respond to the first stage of this proposal."

In this public statement, issued November 21, 1978, the Cuban bishops also supported "the offer presented by the president of the State Council, Fidel Castro" that "guarantees the immediate release of the vast majority of those . . . who for reasons of a political nature are still not free, who, along with their beloved relatives, are anxiously awaiting the time when they can put this painful experience behind them and begin their lives anew."

It was particularly interesting that the bishops, plainly in harmony with the gospel spirit they are called to proclaim, took the initiative of pointing to the dangers involved in visits from those who had left, given the kind of society they were coming from and for which they had opted, and anticipated the mindset they would have, since they could rekindle or create pernicious consumerist aspirations among their relatives and friends in Cuba.

Turning to the Catholic people, the bishops said, "At the same time, we ask our dearly beloved faithful to join us in praying to the Lord and to Our Mother, Our Lady of Charity, invoking their help in this task in which all of us Cubans feel closely bound together, as do all Christians for reasons of faith."

Other churches and Christian ecumenical movements in Cuba made similar statements.[27]

## The Celebration of the Feast of Our Lady of Charity in Havana (1978)

On September 8, 1978, a very significant celebration of the feast of the patroness of Cuba took place in her archdiocesan shrine in Havana. This church had been the starting point for the 1961 procession, which had been broken up and which had such regrettable consequences for the Cuban churches in the years following.[28]

On this new occasion, Archbishop Francisco Oves led the concelebration and the apostolic pronuncio, Archbishop Mario Tagliaferri, preached. Along with the priests of Havana, there were representatives of the revolutionary government and of the diplomatic corps, seminarians from San Carlos, representatives from other parish communities in the archdioceses, and the faithful from that neighborhood.

Those who took part received a card commemorating the event. On it was printed the statement made eighty years before on the occasion of the first Mass celebrated in the old shrine of Our Lady of Charity in El Cobre. That event was organized by the High Command of the Liberating Army of Cuba headed by General Agustín Cabreco Sánchez, in thanksgiving for the independence of Cuba from Spain.

As he spoke the customary final words of gratitude and farewell to those who had taken part, Archbishop Oves made a passing reference to the revolution now taking place in Cuba and called it an event that has "enabled the Cuban people to become aware of their own identity."

The archbishop's carefully chosen words, the presence of representatives of the state and the diplomatic corps in full view of those taking part, and the remembrance of the historic insurrectionary Mass provided an image that blotted out the one left in that same place by the events that had taken place there seventeen years previously. All this served to make evident the changes that had taken place within the Cuban church during the decade launched throughout the Latin American continent by the Medellín Conference, in which a delegation from the church in Cuba had taken part.

## Final Events Closing the Re-encounter Phase and Prefiguring Another

The death of Pope Paul VI led to new expectations in the universal church. It occurred while a new stage in the life of the Latin American church was in preparation, one that would be planned at the Third General Conference of the Latin American Bishops (Puebla, Mexico), which was briefly postponed. Paul VI died just as the opening stage of dialogue between the Cuban church and the revolutionary people of Cuba reached its peak. More than had been the case during the brief pontificate of his immediate predecessor, Pope John Paul I, the election of the Polish cardinal, Karol Wojtyla, as Pope John Paul II produced a situation of uncertainty but one brimming with hope for the Cuban church in view of the novel element in this pontiff: the first pope from a people that was also building socialism.[29]

The Holy See's decision to create the new diocese of Holguín, by separating it from the archdiocese of Santiago de Cuba, of which it was to be a suffragan diocese, satisfied a need and responded to a request that had been presented to Rome for some years. It also restructured the ecclesiastical division of Cuba in a manner helpful to the local church. This was not simply fulfilling a canonical requirement with regard to the increase of the faithful, but was a reasonable concession on the part of the Holy See, which responded to this request from the Cuban church, thus showing its apostolic zeal for that church in these special circumstances. Bishop Héctor Peña Gómez was named first bishop of the new diocese. He had been, in effect, serving in that capacity as auxiliary bishop of Santiago de Cuba since 1971, the year he was ordained a bishop.

Another gesture that also revealed the esteem of the Holy See for the Cuban church and the people of Cuba, and one that was consistent with the repeated messages that successive Roman pontiffs had sent to the local church in the country, especially in more recent years, was the raising to the rank of minor basilica of the national shrine, built in the town of El Cobre, near Santiago de Cuba, and dedicated to Our Lady of Charity, the patroness of Cuba. This took place in January 1979 when Cardinal Gantin was visiting the country. He brought the papal bull and presided over the Mass celebrated in the basilica.

A further indication that one historical period was ending and another was beginning was the fact that Bishop Manuel Rodríguez Rozas of Pinar del Río submitted his resignation for reasons of health to the Holy Father; it was accepted, and the young Cuban priest Jaime Ortega was appointed to replace him. Ortega was ordained a bishop on January 14, 1979, in the cathedral church of the diocese of Matanzas, where he was pastor, and he took possession of the diocese of Pinar del Río on January 21 in the cathedral there.

Another development indicating a transition to a new stage in the history of the Cuban church in its relationship to the new socialist society was the end of the diplomatic activity of Archbishop Mario Tagliaferri as papal pronuncio in Cuba on January 24, 1979, and the appointment of his successor, Archbishop Giuseppe Laigueglia, who came from the nunciature in Bolivia. When he assumed his new duties, Laigueglia already had a reputation as a renewal-oriented and progressive bishop, who was more in tune with the direction of work set by Archbishop Zacchi than that of Tagliaferri.

Finally, the Third General Conference of the Latin American Bishops, held in Puebla, Mexico, in 1979,[30] closed the period that had opened for the church in Latin America ten years before at Medellín. Cuba fully belongs to Latin America by its geographical location, its culture, its past history, and its historic destiny. The Medellín Conference signified a surprising openness on the part of the church in Latin America to the reality of what was happening in contemporary history. Even if it did not satisfy the aspiration of the most impatient, the Puebla Conference took a step forward in the process of "updating" the Latin American church, despite its ambiguities and its hesitancy. Medellín projected an influence that was clearly favorable for the Cuban church, which subsequently began to be reconciled with its own people. Catholics and the Cuban people could have even greater hopes for Puebla if they knew how to translate its basic reflections into the concrete and specific needs of the church in Cuba. The cordial greeting sent by Pope John Paul II to Fidel Castro while the former was flying over Cuban territory on his way back to the Vatican from Mexico was an omen of new and more beneficial fruits of evangelical reconciliation between the Catholic church and the revolutionary people of Cuba.

# 6

# Dialogue (1979–1985)

## The Resignation of Archbishop Oves

Francisco Oves was unquestionably the bishop who showed the clearest, broadest, and deepest understanding of the historic moment through which the church had been living during the Cuban socialist revolution. He was the first member of the hierarchy who understood and taught the harmony possible between many of the gospel principles inspiring Christianity and the scientific foundations that motivate socialism.[1]

However, Oves was unable to lead either the Cuban bishops or the Cuban church in that direction. On the contrary, the pronuncio Tagliaferri's failure to understand[2] and the uncertainty and fears felt by other bishops—both supported by the rejection of, or "apathy" toward, the revolution shown by most regular churchgoers—were factors that came to have a serious effect on the emotional health of the archbishop of Havana. Things reached the point where his pastoral leadership became erratic on some matters. At the Puebla Conference an attempted gesture of conciliation on Oves's part was blocked by various mechanisms, with the approval of the Holy See and backed by CELAM, under the leadership of Archbishop Alfonso López Trujillo.

When he returned to Cuba from Puebla, Oves had, for

practical purposes, lost his authority. For that reason Archbishop Meurice carried to Rome Oves's offer to resign. Rome summoned Oves, who resigned the see of Havana on April 23, 1981, still young but broken. Indeed, Meurice had been functioning as apostolic administrator of Oves's see since February 2, 1980.

None of the bishops wanted to take Oves's place, since that would entail responsibility for dealing more directly with the superiors of religious orders and congregations, with government authorities, and with foreign visitors simply because Havana was the capital.

## Jaime Ortega Appointed to Succeed Oves

Archbishop Meurice's temporary administration of the see of Havana, which he carried on while still retaining his own see of Santiago de Cuba, ended on November 24, 1981,[3] when the Holy See appointed Bishop Jaime Ortega Alamino, who had recently received the see of Pinar del Río. He was the youngest bishop and the one with the least episcopal experience, but he had had a great deal of pastoral experience as parish priest in Jagüey Grande and in the cathedral of Matanzas after his ordination to the priesthood.

Archbishop Jaime Ortega studied for the priesthood at San Alberto Magno Seminary in the diocese of Matanzas and lived in Cuba during the first year of the revolution. When he finished his philosophy courses in 1960, his bishop sent him to Canada to study theology. After finishing his studies he returned to his diocese to do parish work. His ministry was only partly affected when as a young priest he served in the Military Units to Aid Production.[4] The net result was that he developed special qualities that did not fully emerge until he accepted the task of pastoral leadership in Havana in a situation that seemed so difficult to the other bishops, but which he was able to handle with remarkable skill.

## Bishop Giulio Einaudi, New Pronuncio

Archbishop Laigueglia did not last long as apostolic pronuncio in Cuba. Despite his jovial and open nature, he soon returned to

Rome, ostensibly for reasons of health. On September 28, 1980, it was announced that Bishop Giulio Einaudi had been appointed to replace him.[5]

Einaudi was born on February 11, 1928, in Italy, into a family of political figures outstanding in their own country and elsewhere.[6] He was ordained a priest on June 29, 1951, appointed pronuncio in Pakistan in November 1976, and ordained a bishop on January 2, 1977.

Shortly after getting settled in Cuba and familiarizing himself with the situation, the new pronuncio demonstrated clearly his desire to improve church-state relations. In order to follow such a path, he must have received—perhaps even sought, and obtained—precise guidelines from the Vatican Secretariat of State. This showed once more something that some see as a seemingly contradictory set of policies by Pope John Paul II. What he does, however, does not reflect a subjective attitude but, rather, is a reflection of the objective contradictions confronting the universal church throughout the world.

One gesture that was strange for a foreign ambassador, and most unusual for an apostolic nuncio, but very typical of Bishop Einaudi's diplomatic activity, was his attendance at, and participation in, the Christian Convocation of Churches and Ecumenical Movements against United States Intervention in Cuba, Central America, and the Caribbean, held November 14, 1981. The meeting had been organized by the Ecumenical Council of Cuba, which is made up of Protestant churches and ecumenical movements.

In the final statement approved unanimously by all present, the meeting expressed "the astonishment of our whole people and government in the face of the calumnies and threats made by the United States government against us and against other peoples in our region." A call was issued "to all churches, ecclesiastical bodies, and ecumenical organizations, urging—in the name of Christ, Prince of Peace, and guided by the Holy Spirit, Struggler for Justice—that they, united in solidarity with us, now tell the United States government to stop its aggression, intervention, and threats against Cuba and against the peoples of Central America and the Caribbean."

Also present and speaking at this event were Msgr. Carlos Manuel de Céspedes, director of the General Secretariat of the Cuban Bishops Conference and vicar-general of the archdiocese of Havana; the well-known Catholic poet, Eliseo Diego, who had been honored by the revolutionary government; and other well-known figures in the Catholic church. At that time this was an unusual gesture of ecumenical solidarity.

Einaudi's attitude, which was so different from that of Tagliaferri and so similar to what Zacchi had done in his time, foreshadowed the overall changes to take place in the church with regard to the revolution.

## The Hierarchy's Position on United States Threats against Cuba

The new pronuncio's attitude was soon felt in the church hierarchy. At the end of its forty-sixth ordinary assembly, the Cuban Bishops Conference issued a statement addressed to "all priests, religious, seminarians, and the faithful." In it the bishops said:

> As Cubans we share the feelings of our people who do not want to see the blood of their children spilled and who yearn to live in peace. . . . At this moment there is reason to fear not only an overt military action, but also a threat that the blockade might be stepped up, which in itself would constitute a new aggression. . . . With the deep-seated conviction that comes from our faith in the gospel of Jesus Christ, which is from beginning to end a call to love and to peace, we go on record as rejecting any armed attack and any kind of blockade, and we even oppose psychological warfare as inimical to genuine peace.

Finally they joined with the calls of other episcopal bodies of North and Central America and with people in the state and in the government "who propose negotiation as the only valid and truly human solution for this moment of serious crisis on our region. . . . We are convinced that this is the voice of good sense and we hope that there are still those who have enough good sense to listen."[7]

## The Attitude of the Bishops toward the Mariel Boatlift

The distressing series of events that took place in 1980 when some people with guns in hand entered the Peruvian embassy in Havana, seeking diplomatic asylum, cost the life of one of the guards at that office. The subsequent "invasion" of the embassy by people who were mainly antisocial elements seeking to flee the responsibilities that go along with living in Cuba, then led to the exodus of many of these people to the United States from the Cuban port of Mariel, with the acquiescence of the Cuban government and the active support and encouragement of the governments of the United States, Peru, and Costa Rica.

One of the reasons given by the "émigrés" was that, as Catholics, they were persecuted for their religious beliefs, although many also added that they were alleged to be homosexuals and some brazenly admitted that they were criminals. However, the church's reputation suffered less than it had from previous emigrations for political reasons, because the harmonious and growing dialogue with the state had been going on for a long time and Catholics were increasingly a part of the revolutionary process without giving up their Christian faith, and indeed even being motivated by it.

How open the hierarchy was toward the new socialist society being formed was evident in statements made by the bishops and in the explicit guidelines given to pastors and priests so that, in their homilies, they might clearly explain the official attitude of the church at that moment. These guidelines can be summed up as follows:

1. The church is not going to leave Cuba.
2. The church respects the free option of each believer to leave the country.
3. The church exhorts believers to remain in Cuba.

4. The church urges its members to reflect seriously in the light of faith before making a decision that will lead them to leave the country.
5. The church redoubles its efforts to follow out its already formulated guidelines on the participation of Catholics in life in Cuban society and the revolutionary construction of the new society, motivated by their faith.

This attitude reveals not only the continuity of the process of the church's re-encounter with the people, but the unfolding of this process.

## The Impact of the Nicaraguan Sandinista Revolution

From the beginning the Cuban Revolution had an unquestionable influence on the direction taken by political events in Latin America. That influence was in some indirect fashion at work in the Christian renewal in countries like Brazil (Christian base communities), Argentina (Priests for the Third World), Peru (National Office of Social Research – ONIS), and so forth, and more directly in Chile (Christians for Socialism), as well as in Panama, Mexico, Ecuador, and so forth. After the victory of the Sandinista Revolution in Nicaragua, a striking feedback process began.

Prior to 1959 many Catholics and Christians in Cuba and other countries took part in revolutionary struggles for the rights of the people. However, they did so more out of the traditional dichotomy of faith and patriotism that split their consciousness rather than out of a Christian missionary spirit of serving the world. In only a few instances did both factors interrelate, as was the case of the Cuban student leader José Antonio Echeverría and the first priest guerrilla of the twentieth century, *Comandante* Father Guillermo Sardiñas in Cuba.

However, starting in the 1970s, the ever-growing presence of Catholics and other Christians in the continent's liberation struggles demonstrated that the old alienating barriers were being torn down and that Christians, whether Catholics or not, were taking part in these struggles motivated by their faith, which began to be incarnated in new ideologies even when they were materialist, like Marxist ideology.

If on his visits to Chile (1971) and to Jamaica (1977) Fidel explained his position that there should be a "strategic alliance" between Marxists and revolutionary Christians, in Nicaragua, both before and after the revolutionary victory—and despite the subsequent opposition of the Catholic hierarchy and other Christian sectors manipulated by the right wing and imperialism—what emerged was not so much an "alliance" as a certain "unity" between Christians and Sandinista atheists. From that point on, Christian faith could not be seen anymore as an obstacle or the "opium" of peoples, since in growing numbers of believers it was becoming something that was motivating, stimulating, and spurring democratic, and even socialist, revolution.

Hence, Fidel himself, after his visit to Nicaragua for the first anniversary of the Sandinista Revolution, felt prompted to make this acknowledgement before the people of Cuba, gathered to celebrate the twenty-sixth anniversary of the attack on the Moncada barracks:

> In Chile and Jamaica we had spoken about the strategic alliance between Christians and Marxist-Leninists. In Latin America if the revolution were to take on an antireligious character it would lead to the division of the people. . . . The reactionary classes have tried to use religion against progress and against revolution and, in fact, for a long time they were successful; but times change and it is increasingly difficult for imperialism, the oligarchy, and reactionary forces to use the church against revolution.
>
> Many religious leaders no longer talk only about the goods of the other world and happiness in the by-and-by. They are talking about needs in this world and happiness in this world. . . . If we take into account that initially the Christian religion was the religion of the poor, . . . because it was based on deeply human precepts, there is no question that the revolutionary movement, the socialist movement, the communist movement, the Marxist-Leninist movement would gain a great deal to the extent

> that upright leaders in the Catholic church and other churches were to return to the Christian spirit of the age of the slaves in Rome. . . . In fact, I believe not only would socialism and communism benefit, but Christianity would also come out ahead.
>
> Some religious leaders in Nicaragua said to us, "Why 'strategic alliance'?" and "Why just a 'strategic alliance'?" "Why not talk about unity between Marxist-Leninists and Christians?" . . . I am quite convinced that such a formula is highly explosive.[8]

All of this, plus the constant movement of doctors, nurses, teachers, construction workers, both believers and nonbelievers, to Nicaragua on missions of international solidarity, indirectly served to speed the process of wiping out the taboo that had taken root in Cuba (to the satisfaction of imperialism and the counterrevolution) due to the prejudices built up over time and political confrontations during the first years of the revolution, on the part of both believers and atheists.

## The International Context of the Gradual Thaw

Besides previous events in Chile and throughout Latin America, the impact of the Sandinista Revolution, the struggle of the Salvadoran people, and so forth, the influence, on Cuba, of events taking place elsewhere should not be ignored.

It should be noted that the thinking of the Catholic church in Cuba was significantly influenced by the CELAM Conference held in Puebla at the end of the 1970s. Although less progressive than the Medellín Conference of the 1960s, Puebla had more influence within Cuba.

Despite its censures of Marxist atheism, economic collectivism, and so forth, the Catholic design set forth at the Puebla Conference found greater welcome in socialist Cuba than in other countries of the region because of its numerous statements on behalf of the poor, the development of peoples, free schooling, public health, and other things to which people aspired, and which were recognized as already existing in an exemplary way in Cuba.

Through the work of the hierarchy and clergy, certain papal documents—all from John Paul II—also had positive effects in Cuba: the encyclicals *Redemptor Hominis,* March 4, 1979 (although in Cuba it was studied years later), *Dives in Misericordia,* November 30, 1979, and to an even greater extent *Laborem Exercens,* September 14, 1981, as well as the Apostolic Exhortation *Familiaris Consortio,* November 22, 1981. In addition, John Paul II's messages for the yearly Days of Prayer for Peace, his speeches and homilies during his various trips, and especially his speech to the Cuban bishops during their *ad limina* visit on June 30, 1983, were all influential in Cuba.[9]

A favorable trend from another source during these years was at work in various international and regional meetings of communist and worker parties, such as those of Central America, Panama and Mexico, whose published statements dealt, among other topics, with the area of religion from a new viewpoint. That not only helped party-related social sectors to open themselves to dialogue but made it easier for the church to enter into the process.

## The Second Congress of the Communist Party of Cuba

Such was the national and international context for the celebration of the Second Congress of the Communist Party of Cuba in December 1980. Although many of its resolutions did no more than ratify and press for a continuation of the policies laid out at the First Congress held in 1975, the resolution on the policy toward religion, the church, and believers, which repeated the classic assessment of religion, also showed a greater recognition of positive activity by Christians no longer just in mainland Latin America but in Cuba itself.

> . . . the socialist state and the government have maintained normal and satisfactory relationships with the vast majority of the religious institutions located in our country.
>
> The normal functioning of worship by each denomination or creed, the holding of meetings, assemblies, conferences, and other activities typical of religious institutions and associations and groups of believers, including the

> celebration of international religious events, eloquently demonstrate that this policy is being carried out, . . . as does the increasing interchange of delegations of representatives of religious denominations and Cuban lay people who travel elsewhere and those from other countries who come to our own for religious purposes and for those of social justice and of peace.

The Second Congress also urged that "there be greater participation by the whole population, believing and non-believing, in the building of socialism," and that "believers with different religious viewpoints be brought ever more fully into the revolutionary tasks of building socialism."

The congress took Fidel's well-known position on the Christian-Marxist "strategic alliance" so far as to proclaim the need for "joint unified action with progressive and revolutionary sectors (in the churches), aimed at really attaining social progress, peace, and the building of a new and more just society."[10]

These public statements continued to make an effective contribution toward loosening the remaining tensions in church-state relations in Cuba. Consequently, there was a lessening of discrimination against Christians in the spheres of labor, administration, and government—and less rejection of the revolution in ecclesiastical circles, although neither entirely disappeared.[11]

## The Cuban Bishops' *Ad Limina* Visit

During the second half of June 1983, the Cuban bishops went to Rome for their canonical *ad limina* visit to Pope John Paul II. While in Rome they visited several departments of the Roman Curia, met with different ecclesiastical figures, and met separately with the pope on the twenty-seventh and the thirtieth of June. He received them as a group on the latter day in a meeting that was described as "friendly" *(familiar)*.[12]

During his meeting with the group, Pope John Paul II delivered a speech in Spanish, praising them, the Cuban clergy, religious, and laity, and the country's Catholic community as a whole. The pope emphasized the need for the church, especially through the laity, to have "an active presence in society" in Cuba. He told them:

> I know that you, the bishops of the church in Cuba, have a deep appreciation for the laudable contribution made by so many lay people who are conscious of the demands laid on them by baptism and are committed to various responsibilities in the church. I also know that you give full importance to the active presence of those lay people in the social tasks of your context. . . . Today my voice seeks to be united to yours so as to express to the Catholic laity of Cuba in the name of Christ my wholehearted recognition of their sense of ecclesial and social consciousness. . . . Thus I unite my desire to your own so as to encourage a greater active lay presence in the life of society, while taking care to preserve their Catholic identity.[13]

The pope mentioned the family, and deplored divorce, "which is unfortunately so common, whose roots are to be found in lack of thought before marriage, unwillingness to persevere in commitment, the separation of spouses due to work, housing shortages, and other reasons," such as abortion.[14] The church is willing to help resolve such social problems.

The pope emphasized that Catholic faith is "a positive and unifying element in the cultural identity and independence of the Cuban nation" because it has been "actively present in the history of the Cuban people. It has been active since the very beginning of Cuban national identity, with outstanding figures like Father Félix Varela."[15]

The pope sent greetings to the "Cuban Church in Reflection," which was taking place during those years in our country. The purpose was to seek greater sharing between church and people during this revolutionary phase of its history. The pope said that the church, "in this sense, is open to dialogue with society, and it also appreciates all the signs of collaboration and good will it receives from the authorities of the nation."[16] For that purpose he expressed his desire that the church in Cuba enjoy the "scope of freedom it needs in order to further the cause of the welfare and the deep yearnings of the people, of which it joyfully knows that it is a part and a collaborator, from the standpoint of its own mission."[17]

The pope's tone, demanding but also conciliatory, contrasted with the one he had used a few months before in Nicaragua during his visit to Central America.

## The "Cuban Church in Reflection"

Stimulated by these events that were taking place inside Cuba and elsewhere during this period 1979–85, small groups of seminarians and young priests and religious began to show a certain concern. Directly or indirectly prompted by some lay people, and even by visitors from other countries, they felt that their spirituality, activity, and pastoral mission in Cuba were being challenged. Those taking part in the meetings of these spontaneous groups, at first very few, but more as time went on, came to the point of holding meetings or sharing sessions on their own in a way that was initially very timid, informal, and exploratory.

The concern of some students in San Carlos Seminary was welcomed by Father René David, a French missionary who had come to serve the church in Cuba during the revolution. He had been a teacher at the seminary in Havana for many years. As a result of his reflection together with these young people, Father David wrote a document titled "Christian Reflection toward a Theology and Pastoral Work of Reconciliation in Cuba." His spirituality was centered on the kind of communion that should exist with God and with all of one's brothers and sisters, whether believers or not. When translated in practical terms into a service that is based on God's love for God's creation, it should lead to the reconciliation of the human family and to overcoming the contradictions that come from lack of love and from sin. This document raises the possibility of "reconciliation between Christians and communists," and what each side can expect of the other.

When this document of "Christian Reflection" had been circulated, discussed, and criticized by a wider circle of Catholics, some seminarians along with young priests and religious presented their primary concerns and conclusions to the bishops.

A favorable reception by the bishops could lead to planning for a joint pastoral work suitable for the situation in Cuba. Hence it was that in the annual gathering of priests held in El Cobre in 1979 and 1980, a unanimous feeling arose that the church in Cuba needed to reflect seriously and in community fashion on its mission in the new socialist society. Bishop Fernando Azcárate, the former auxiliary bishop of Havana, called this necessary reflection "a Cuban Puebla," and he accepted the proposal and backed it with his authority.

In August 1980 the Cuban Bishops Conference created a commission, headed by Bishop Adolfo Rodríguez of Camagüey, to sponsor and lead what came to be called the "Cuban Church in Reflection," or REC *(Reflexión Eclesial Cubana).* On April 19, 1981, the commission resolved to "place the church in a state of reflection on its being and activity in the world in the past, the present, and the future, so as to lead to a National Cuban Ecclesial Convocation (ENEC; Encuentro Nacional Eclesial Cubano) in which some pastoral options might be made." There were representatives from all local communities, whether of parish or diocese and from religious, laity, and hierarchy.

A Preparatory Commission was set up in September 1982, made up of priests, religious, and lay people, and headed by Bishop Azcárate. There were three subcommissions, dealing with history, sociological surveys, and theology. In February 1983 the Preparatory Commission became the Central Commission, headed by Archbishop Ortega of Havana, and set up its office in San Carlos Seminary.

In September the Central Commission stated that "the church in Cuba wants to be renewed and to put itself at the service of *Communion* with God and with that people of which it forms a part." A small working group was given the task of drawing up a draft to be discussed and improved in all Catholic communities in the country. The results of these discussions were subsequently consolidated in diocesan assemblies held throughout the country in April and June 1985.

In August 1985 the Central Commission appointed a Drafting Commission, which, by drawing together all the ideas from the grass roots, was to prepare a Working Document to serve as the focus of discussion in the National Convocation that had been planned. The Working Document was finished in November of that year.[18] With that in mind, the Central Commission issued invitations to the ENEC, to be celebrated in Havana from February 17 to 23 (ten days after the celebration of the Third Congress of the Communist Party in Cuba, a circumstance that turned out to be very significant for the growing dialogue between church and state in Cuba).

The scope, depth, and extreme importance of this conference was foreshadowed not only by the kind of representation coming from the delegates chosen by communities throughout the country, but also by the topics dealt with in the Working Document. The "Cuban Church in Reflection," and its flowering in the convocation, was destined to be the most important Catholic event of the church in Cuba throughout its history. The way in which preparations for it were made, and because it was taking place in a social context with special ideological and political characteristics and in which mutual harmony seemed so pronounced, ensured the importance of the undertaking. This meeting might usher in a new period in the history of the Catholic church in Cuba.

## Acknowledgment of Social Work Done by Sisters

Within the process in which the church and the people were re-encountering one another were many signs of this renewed attitude on the part of the church, which advanced step by step with a growing recognition on the part of the people and similarly on the part of civil authorities in the country.[19]

One such sign, the more noticeable because it continued despite all the misunderstandings and problems, was the wholehearted attitude of service maintained by some communities of religious, such as the Daughters of Charity, the Little Sisters of Disabled Old People (who serve the Santovenia old people's home), the Servants of Mary, Ministers of the Sick, and the Sisters of St. Joseph (who work in homes for children and old people)—all of whom cared for the sick and took care of the other social works of the church.

A well-known example of the impact of this Christian witness—one far more understandable in the new Cuban society than elsewhere—took place in the July 1984 session of the National Assembly of People's Power. Under discussion was the state's proposal to broaden the network of old people's homes throughout the country. Fidel, as a representative in the assembly, asked the one giving the report if he had checked into the high level of quality and effectiveness in both human and economic terms provided by sisters in the church's old people's homes. He then praised their work to the Cuban parliament.[20]

Developments like this one continued to advance the thaw in an atmosphere in which religion had become taboo for many. Later on Fidel told the Brazilian Dominican, Frei Betto, "the Sisters of Charity and other orders, besides doing their work with a great deal of love, are very demanding in the way they use resources. They use things sparingly and the institutions they administer are very economical."[21]

## Rumors of a Possible Papal Visit to Cuba

When Pope John Paul II visited Mexico just before CELAM's Third Conference (Puebla, 1979), Fidel Castro, as head of the Cuban state, visited the pronuncio Tagliaferri in the nunciature in Havana in order personally to offer the hospitality of the people and government of Cuba to His Holiness, should he desire to visit, rest in our country, or land there for technical reasons.

On that occasion the Vatican Secretariat of State replied that, on his way back to Rome, the pope would prefer to land in the Bahamas, the first land Columbus touched before "discovering" Cuba. Word went around that Pope Wojtyla—perhaps for very Polish reasons—did not want to make any discrimination between those Catholic Cubans who had remained in Cuba and those who had gone to Miami. In any case, the invitation was later confirmed by the archbishop of Havana, the pronuncio Einaudi,[22] and Fidel himself.[23]

In his talks with Frei Betto, Fidel had this to say about Pope John Paul II:

> Frankly, I admit we were not very happy that time when the pope did not make a brief stop in our country. Of

> course, that did not prevent us from insisting and repeating our invitations for the pope to visit Cuba. . . . In some recent questions put to the pope, and his answers, one can detect some interest in making contact with our people. . . . We are honored by any interest on the part of the pope in visiting our country, no question about that. In fact, we see it as a brave act, since not . . . just any political figure dares to visit Cuba. Heads of state and politicians have to take very seriously the viewpoint of the United States. Many of them are aware of that, and they fear economic and political reprisals; they are afraid of displeasing the United States. . . . To visit Cuba really becomes a manifestation of independence. And of course, we unquestionably regard the Vatican as an institution or a state with a high idea of independence, but even so we still appreciate the courage entailed in a visit to our country. . . . I am utterly convinced that a visit from the pope would be useful and positive for the church, for Cuba and, I believe, useful for the third world, and would be useful for all countries in many respects.[24] . . .
>
> A visit from the pope would not be mere diplomatic formality. We would undoubtedly discuss all the questions of interest to the pope with regard to the church in Cuba, to Catholics in Cuba. . . . For our part, I would say that our country's basic interest would be connected to the analysis of those questions that are of greatest interest to the underdeveloped countries of Latin America, Asia, and Africa. . . . and of course a meeting with the pope in our country would also have to deal with those problems that are of great interest for all of humankind, such as those related to the arms race and peace.[25]

Concluding his thoughts on a possible visit by the pope, Fidel said:

> Taking all these things into consideration, especially peace, I think there could be a very useful, fruitful, interesting, serious dialogue between the pope and ourselves. I say this because of our respect for the Vatican, our respect for the

> Holy See, our respect for the Catholic church, for in no way do we underestimate it. I have no doubt that in these circumstances a visit by the pope to our country would be extremely significant and I regard it as quite possible.[26]

These assessments from the head of a Communist party in power and of a state within the world socialist community are noteworthy both for the church and its visible head, and for other socialist countries where millions of Catholics live, such as Czechoslovakia and the Baltic republics of the USSR. Even more interesting would be an answer from the pope to these insistent invitations to visit for the first time a socialist country different from his native land.[27]

## A Visit to Cuba by Archbishop Jean Vilnet

In the spring of 1984 Archbishop Jean Vilnet of Lille, France, president of the French Bishops Conference, and Bishop Michel Raymond, general secretary of the conference, visited Cuba. Archbishop Vilnet visited our country with a very unusual and interesting task: that of formally donating to the Cuban government a large sum of money for the purpose of helping finance the Cuban government's plans to set up and develop the national network of special schools for hearing impaired and handicapped children, in line with UNESCO's proposal. This contribution came from the Catholic Committee against Hunger and Underdevelopment in France, which is maintained by the voluntary contributions of French Catholics. What was unusual about the gesture, given the economic blockade against Cuba by capitalist countries, was that it was a free gift from the Catholic church in France, not to its sister church in Cuba, but to the revolutionary Cuban government, and was thus an expression of confidence in its humanitarian purposes. Archbishop Jaime Ortega of Havana hosted the delegation of the French church in the name of the Bishops Conference of Cuba, which had invited them. They met with the Cuban minister of education, José Ramón Fernández, and with the vice president of the Councils of State and of Ministers of Cuba, Carlos Rafael Rodríguez.

This was reported in *Granma,* the official organ of the Central Committee of Cuba's Communist party, on May 10, 1984.

## An Ecumenical Meeting with the Rev. Jesse Jackson

Ecumenical relations, which on the Catholic side had been frozen since the late 1960s, began to thaw at the highest level of the hierarchy when in June 1984 the American Baptist minister, the Rev. Jesse Jackson, visited Cuba at the invitation of the Baptist church in Cuba on the occasion of the anniversary of the murder of the Rev. Martin Luther King, Jr.

In Cuba the Rev. Mr. Jackson met with Fidel Castro, and together they held an extensive press conference that was shown on Cuban television. Together they attended the main celebration in honor of Martin Luther King, which was held in the largest Cuban Methodist church. The spirit was that of the broadest ecumenical feeling yet seen in Cuba, with the top leadership of both Protestant and Catholic churches and of the state and the party all in attendance.[28]

Officially representing the Catholic church in Cuba were Archbishop Jaime Ortega Alamino, vice president of the Bishops Conference, Msgr. Carlos Manuel de Céspedes, the head of the Permanent Secretariat of the conference, among other figures from the Catholic clergy and laity.

## Commemoration of Father Sardiñas's Death

On December 21, 1983, in the Cristóbal Colón Cemetery in Havana, there was a ceremony marking the nineteenth anniversary of the death of the first Latin American priest guerrilla of the twentieth century, and the one with the highest military rank, Father Guillermo Sardiñas, a member of the Rebel Army of Cuba that overthrew the tyranny of Fulgencio Batista. The event was organized by the Cuban Institute of Friendship with Peoples. Important figures from the party, the state, and the Christian churches in Cuba took part.

A year later, on the twentieth anniversary, the ceremony was given even more importance. Cuba's flag waved alongside the headstone marking the site of Father Sardiñas's grave, surrounded with floral wreaths sent by various figures and institutions in society and the church, and most notably one sent by Fidel Castro. Present at the ceremony were Juan Almeida Bosque, revolutionary commander and member of the Political Bureau of the party; Jesús Montané, head of the Department of International Relations of the Central Committee; other high party figures; also Archbishop Jaime Ortega of Havana, vice president of the Bishops Conference; Msgr. Carlos M. de Céspedes, head of the Permament Secretariat; other important figures from among the Catholic laity, from the Ecumenical Council of Cuba and its member churches; and members of ecumencial movements. The words of remembrance were given by Jorge Enrique Mendoza, the editor of *Granma,* member of the Central Committee of the party, and captain in the Rebel Army, who praised *Comandante* Sardiñas's patriotism as well as his priestly Christian witness during the war for liberation and afterward.[29]

The ceremony was celebrated in similar circumstances a year later, and became a tradition. Ricardo Alarcón, the vice minister of foreign affairs, gave the speech on the twentieth anniversary of Father Sardiñas's entry into the pantheon of the heroes of our country.

## Mutual Visits by United States and Cuban Bishops

From January 21–25, 1985, a delegation from the Bishops Conference of the United States visited Cuba. Heading it was Bishop James Malone of Youngstown, Ohio, the president of the conference. The delegation also included Archbishop Bernard Law of Boston, Archbishop Patricio Flores of San Antonio, Monsignor Daniel Hoye, the general secretary of the conference, and Father David Gallivan, of the Secretariat for Latin America.[30]

This gesture, which was consistent with the pastoral letter on war and peace published two years previously by the bishops of the United States, was basically an act of family solidarity from the church in the United States to its sister church in Cuba. But it inevitably entailed an acknowledgment of the political status of the Cuban people constructing a socialist society, which even though it did not mean approval of that socialist aim, did express at least a new realistic openness. One sign was the fact that the visitors did not limit themselves simply to meetings and establishing bonds with the bishops and with Cuban Catholic circles; they also had important meetings with the head of state, Fidel Castro, and with other Cuban government and party figures. This was publicized in the national newspaper.[31]

In a press interview after the visit, the archbishop of Havana said that the American church leaders "have become receptive and understand the situation of our church and of our society in Cuba. They have done so looking at us not as judges or analysts, but as pastors of the church who always try to discover in the people everything that can unite human beings, that can improve life ever more in the future."[32]

During the visit, the American bishops acknowledged the "remarkable improvement" in educational and cultural levels among the people; the "noticeable increase in health care, evident in the low rate of infant mortality"; and the "real but limited" progress being made in church-state relations. In this connection they indicated the "need for an active and organized dialogue" between church and state authorities and they noted Fidel Castro's openness to the idea.

The American bishops also said that they had raised the question of the reunification of families of Cuban origin who live in the United States and have relatives in Cuba serving sentences for counterrevolutionary crimes. They said further that they had presented a list of names, with the hope that these people and others who had finished their sentences might leave the country. They also discussed with the Cuban authorities possibilities for trips between Cuba and the United States by Cubans and others and what would be required financially. To the press they said that they had the impression that there is a desire for normalization of relations between Cuba and the United States. Naturally that would include halting the blockade.[33]

As an outgrowth of this visit, two months later a delegation of Cuban bishops paid a reciprocal visit to the United States. It was significant—and an expression of the new atmosphere of dialogue that was developing throughout this period—that, by way of the Cuban bishops, Fidel Castro personally sent messages to the American bishops about the matters they had discussed in Cuba. In order to do this, Castro met personally with the Cuban bishops. As a result of these meetings between the Cuban bishops and Fidel Castro, it was agreed that they would soon have a working meeting, although no date was set. That meeting took place later that year, in November.[34]

### The Communist Party's Office for Attending to Religious Affairs Made a Separate Department; Homage by the Churches to Dr. Carneado

Another sign, although not ecclesiastical, was directly related to the churches in Cuba and showed the growing interest of the Cuban state and the Communist party in improving their relations with the churches. That was the agreement reached on January 31, 1985, in the Eleventh Extraordinary Plenum of the Central Committee of the Communist party, which was informed of and approved the decision of its Political Bureau. According to that decision, the Office for Attending to Religious Affairs, which had been functioning as a subdepartment of the Department of Science, Culture, and Teaching Centers of the Central Committee, was linked directly to the Secretariat of the Central Committee, headed personally by the first secretary, Fidel Castro. It was given the rank of an independent department, and Dr. José Felipe Carneado, who had headed it when it was a subdepartment, was put in charge and given the rank of department head.[35]

In both party and church circles in Cuba this was interpreted as an important step toward intensifying the dialogue and constructive exchange between church and state. In confirmation of this assessment, there were some bitter criticisms from sectors against the revolution who live in the United States, those who are opposed to any kind of harmonizing of interests among the Cuban people, of which the church is a part.

Similarly significant and in relative contrast to what has just been mentioned, was the seventieth birthday homage that the Catholic Bishops Conference paid to Dr. Carneado privately in the nunciature in July 1985. The Ecumenical Council also offered a more public act of homage, with representatives from all its member churches and movements, and others as well, including the Catholic church. Since there were Catholics, Protestants, Jews, and atheists present, this was seen as the most fully ecumenical event thus far except for the homage to the memory of the Rev. Martin Luther King, Jr., held earlier in Havana.[36]

## Church Presence in Discussions on the Foreign Debt

In this atmosphere of growing communication between church and state in Cuba, the first instance of relatively straightforward collaboration from the perspective of each side, and one that augurs well for future possibilities, was the public participation of an official delegation of the Catholic hierarchy, alongside delegations from other Christian churches, in the international meetings held in Havana, starting in mid-1985. They met together to consider the very serious problem that the foreign debt represents for Latin American and Caribbean peoples, and for the rest of the third world—indeed, for everyone on earth. Possible solutions were discussed.

These conferences, sponsored by the Cuban government—or more precisely by its head, Fidel Castro—had an impact around the world as they fostered a worldwide process of thinking and searching. The Cuban church, which in previous years had absented itself from any activity that even remotely could have political implications, in this grave time did not hesitate to offer both its presence in solidarity and its direct ethical message. Bishop Adolfo Rodríguez, the president of the Cuban Bishops Conference; Archbishop Jaime Ortega, the vice president; and Msgr. Carlos M. de Céspedes, the head of the office of its Permament Committee, constituted a highest-level church delegation to the Dialogue of Continent-Level Figures on the issue.

Some weeks earlier, at the Meeting of Youth, the Catholic church was represented by the young Father José Félix Pérez, rector of San Carlos Seminary; a young Sister of Charity; and three young lay people, male and female, and of different occupations.

It had been agreed that the Cuban delegates to these events would ensure that the foreigners had opportunity to speak in public, which they did. Nevertheless, the Cubans strongly made their presence felt, and the statements made by Archbishop Ortega revealed the position of the Cuban church. The same was true of the statement that Bishop Adolfo Rodríguez sent to the faithful of his diocese, which the Bishops Conference made its own under the title "Guidelines of the Church Magisterium on the Foreign Debt and the New International Economic Order."

The Cuban bishops said:

> . . . it is not up to the church to do away with the International Monetary Fund (IMF) with a stroke of the pen, nor to draw up legislation on a country's exports and imports, nor to close the World Bank and put its employees out of work, nor to fix prices for raw materials and manufactured products.

However,

> because this problem of the foreign debt is a problem of moral responsibility, the church cannot remain neutral, as though if it did so, the issue would thereby not be moral. . . . Nothing human can be foreign to the church; it is not an expert in economics, but it is an expert in humanity.
>
> Prior to being structural, sins are personal. . . . The blind forces of nature . . . may intervene, but they are not always the cause. Injustices are produced by human beings, and human beings can and must correct them. The foreign debt is a complex phenomenon brought about by economic dependence. . . . any aid that creates dependence does not liberate but, rather, subjects, humiliates, insults, and impoverishes.
>
> . . . Latin America has come to its worst economic crisis in this century. It is impossible to develop a country under these conditions. . . . The whole continent has become, as John Paul II says, a giant mirror reflecting "the unfolding of the parable of the rich glutton and the poor Lazarus," who are separated by an enormous chasm.

. . . Everyone rejects the solutions proposed by the International Monetary Fund, because they consist of sharp adjustments, which moreover are unfair, since they fall exclusively on the backs of the debtors and not on the creditors. . . . The church's magisterium teaches that economics cannot be separated from morality because in that case it becomes inhuman. . . . For a long time, indeed, the church has been urging that there be a new economic order, on both national and international levels. . . .

At the conference held in Havana one could observe a consensus that the crisis caused by the foreign debt is very serious and immediate; that the debt cannot be paid under present conditions; that the IMF's solutions must be rejected; that Latin America must be integrated; and that there is an urgent need for a New International Economic Order. . . . Another significant fact about the conference was the temporal commitment of so many Latin American Christians attending the meeting. It is sometimes said that faith alienates, seeks escape, and prevents people from being committed; that faith destroys their responsibility for history and points them toward a nonexistent world; that religion is antiscience and is a private affair. These Christians, however, showed us that in their very faith, and growing out of their very faith, they find an internal drive and further motivation for their commitment to humankind and to society. Without compromising their conscience, their dignity, and their autonomy, they make faith in God the ultimate basis for this very conscience, autonomy, and dignity.

The lay people of our dioceses are not indifferent or insensitive toward this problem or toward any other human problem. . . . Cuban lay people, in their work, study, and professional life, through their commitment and example, are in no way different from those Christians whom we saw and got to know during the conference.[37]

### *Fidel and Religion*

The last manifestation—somewhat unexpected but quite noteworthy—in this higher or deeper level of dialogue between the socialist state and the Catholic church in Cuba was the publication in late 1985, first in Brazil and soon afterward in Cuba, of conversations between Fidel Castro and the Brazilian Dominican, Frei Betto, under the title *Fidel and Religion.*[38]

In this book Betto wrote down not only the many personal, family, and political experiences that Fidel described. Betto also explained that, despite the admiration and respect he showed for the moral precepts learned in the Catholic schools where he studied in his youth, Fidel had noted that education was not able to awaken Christian faith in him. Nevertheless—and this is remarkable in such confessions—the leader of the Cuban Revolution showed that he was pleasantly surprised, as a Marxist-Leninist, to see the growing involvement of Latin American Christians in the liberation struggles of their peoples now, under the impulse of a faith, made explicit in what is known as liberation theology and manifested in a side-by-side struggle with their atheist brothers and sisters who are motivated by ideologies foreign to Christian faith. Up to this point, Fidel had not added anything new to his well-known position on the "strategic alliance" between Christians and Marxists, except for acknowledging and applauding the fact that it was more and more being put into concrete political practice.

Perhaps more novel was the respectful way Fidel spoke about the Apostolic Roman See, and more specifically about the efforts for peace made by Pope John Paul II. Even more interesting in the Cuban context was Fidel's acknowledgment that, contrary to the official policy of the party and the state, in Cuba there have been some subtle and not wholly justifiable discriminations against Christians. (He also makes it clear, however, that religion in Cuba has been used as a "counterrevolutionary weapon.") Further, he urges that activists in both the party and the church in Cuba should struggle to overcome the conditions that cause such discriminations and divisions between the party and the church.[39]

Particularly interesting is Fidel's opinion on religion, judging from a political viewpoint. He believes that Marx's dictum that "religion is the opium of the people" may have had historic value and have been absolutely correct at a particular moment, but that religion in itself is neither an opiate nor a wonderful cure.

It may be either opium or cure to the extent it is used or applied to defend either oppressors and exploiters or oppressed and exploited.

The most important element in this book is the outright openness shown by the head of a Communist party in power and of a socialist state toward the unquestionably impressive phenomenon of Christian renewal taking place in Latin America, which is beginning to influence the church universal, although not without contradictions. The ideas Fidel expressed to Betto might be surprising to those who have only the disinformation on the Cuban Revolution spread by its enemies, but it is not surprising to those who have followed firsthand or who have experienced from the inside the ideological-political process taking place in Cuba through the socialist revolution.[40]

## End of Another Period or of a Whole Era?

In this study of its relations with the socialist state and government and with the Cuban people as it is fully engaged in the revolutionary building of socialism in the country, the church has been treated more as a social institution, which it is, than in its intrinsic nature as a divine institution. It has likewise been seen materially as the community of believers. At this stage those relations reached a level of dialogue that largely overcame the mistrust, antagonism, and tension of previous stages and seemed to prefigure that in the future collaboration would be possible and even necessary. Such a relationship based on a mutually honest and respectful critical acceptance could benefit both sides.

The imminence of the Third Congress of the Cuban Communist party, which would no doubt make some statements about the churches and believers, and of ENEC, both of which were to take place in February 1986, to be followed soon afterward by the assemblies of the Ecumenical Council of Cuba, and of other Christian churches and ecumenical movements, gave the impression that one era was over and a new one was beginning, one in which intercommunication could be even more positive and more intense. What the party called "participation or integration of believers into the tasks of the revolution in order to build socialism" and what the Catholic church regarded as "communion with that people of which it is a part" might develop much more fruitfully.

Laws as important for both society and church as the law on worship and religious institutions, which would complement the 1976 Constitution seemed to be near promulgation by the state so as to normalize and stabilize those relationships in a long-term way.

More than simply a new phase, it could be that a whole new era in the history of the church, and perhaps of Cuba itself, might be opening, the period in which the church would be incorporated into the building of the new socialist society. The church is here understood institutionally, since as community many of its members have been taking on this task of participation, or "communion," on their own for many years, despite the suspicion and mistrust they had suffered in one circle or another. It might happen that from now on they and many others would continue to be involved, motivated by their faith and as an apostolate of love and service, but without suffering any discrimination from society or censures from the church.

Perhaps for the sake of both the Cuban people and the whole world, the prophetic lines of the heroic guerrilla *Comandante* Ernesto (Che) Guevara would come true:

> Christians must opt for revolution once for all, especially on our continent where Christian faith is so important within the mass of the people. However, in the revolutionary struggle Christians cannot seek to impose their own dogmas to proselytize for the churches. When they come they should not seek to evangelize Marxists, nor should they out of cowardice hide their faith in order to be more like them. When Christians dare to provide wholehearted revolutionary witness, the revolution will be invincible, for up to now Christians have allowed their teaching to be utilized by reactionaries.[41]

# 7

# Conclusions

This modest contribution to the study of the role played by the Catholic church in the recent history of the Cuban people reveals some of the contradictions that dialectically energize the development of society and its institutions. The aim of this work has not been to provide a definitive chapter in the history of Cuba, but to take a simple look at one of its less studied aspects, that of the imprint of the church on the revolutionary movement of the people and of that movement on the church.

An exclusively "earthly" way of looking at this counterpoint between church and society in this period (and the same is true of the previous periods in Cuban history) can lead to very different assessments of the church.

For some, the church's ability to adapt to the environment in which it lives and develops might be seen as a kind of mimicry, and they would not hesitate to call it opportunism. Others would see this as a surprising and perhaps admirable vitality. However, few would stop to reflect how, from a purely sociological viewpoint, the internal contradictions that have appeared in the church since its foundation (already in the apostolic age, then in conflicts between religious orders, then between them and the papacy, and between the laity and the clergy, and in more modern times between the clergy and the hierarchy) have enabled it to move forward and rise above schisms, splits, and breakaway movements. These contradictions, schisms, divisions, and breakaway movements within the church are reflections of the splits in the social formation in which the church has taken root or of which it has formed a part, and all of them have helped bring the church into dialogue with these social formations in a mutual challenge that has taken very different forms. This is an undeniable fact, which the Catholic church exemplifies more than any other social institution, no matter what one might want to demonstrate or emphasize by it.

We Catholics who strive to configure our lives to the example of Jesus and what he was striving to do in history contemplate this phenomenon in the light of faith, which, far from constricting rational analysis, stimulates, expands, and illuminates it. Through faith, we discover that this adaptability on the part of the church, despite the opportunism and other sins of its members at all levels, is its sacramental sign and its mystery; a perceptible sign of its origin and ongoing inspiration by the Spirit of God; a mystery insofar as it has been unique and unequaled throughout human history, even if that can be explained sociologically. Christ's statement, "The gates of hell will not prevail against it" (which should be translated: "the power of death will not be equal to it"), has proved true up to the present despite all that we members of his Body have been able to do to nullify his saving mission. Its Head, Christ, according to Paul's image, has led the church to live and even give life, above and beyond the deadly influence of its own sinful members and even of its enemies.

During the period of Cuban history in which I have tried to consider the attitude of the Catholic church, these internal and external contradictions have been brought out, as has their dialectical nature. Starting with mistrust and then opposition, the church in Cuba went through a time of marginalization and then passed on to a re-encounter with the people, which, with an intensified dialogue, prefigures a reintegration and possible collaboration in which an orthopractice may lead to a higher level of orthodoxy. The same may be said of the Cuban people, government, state, and Communist party, with which the church as institution is interrelated and forms part of some of their institutions. That may be even more true at longer range, as has been the case in previous instances in history. This rapprochement is not a chance occurrence.

The problem, however, is not one of survival but of meaning.

Christ, who lived in the world "to serve and not to be served," placed his friends, disciples, and followers in the church to continue his work of liberation, justice, love, and peace until the end of time. That means fitting the good news, or gospel, to each local or historical situation, to each culture, to each social formation. All too often, we, his followers, have betrayed this mission, which has nevertheless continued to be carried out with the shifts that are naturally to be expected. One of these cycles of recovery seems to be taking place now in Cuba. The Catholic church is striving to rescue its tradition of service to the people, which in the past has been represented by Bartolomé de las Casas, Espada y Landa, Father Caballero, and Félix Varela, to name only a few of its more illustrious children who, with great effort and sacrifice, played a role in forging this country.

At Vatican Council II the universal church has acknowledged that it "gratefully understands that in its community life no less than in its individual children, it receives a variety of helps from people of every rank and condition. . . . Indeed, the church admits that it has greatly profited and still profits from the antagonism of those who oppose or persecute her" (*Gaudium et Spes,* no. 44). The official voice of the church has not always been so humbly honest, as befits its origin and mission. What now needs to happen is that, in this spirit, the church some day bring those who oppose it to make a similar confession and express similar gratitude. That is our modest aspiration as Cuban Catholics. Amen.

# Acronyms and Short Forms

| | |
|---|---|
| ASO | Organized Lay Apostolate (Apostolado Seglar Organizado) |
| CEC | Ecumenical Council of Cuba (Consejo Ecuménico de Cuba) |
| CEHILA | Commission for Research into Latin American Church History (Comisión de Estudios de Historia de la Iglesia en Latinoamérica) |
| CELAM | Latin American Bishops Council (Consejo Episcopal Latinoamericano) |
| CENDESEC | Center for Ecumenical Studies (Centro de Estudios Ecuménicos) |
| CIA | Central Intelligence Agency |
| CTC | Cuban Workers Federation (Central de Trabajadores de Cuba) |
| ENEC | National Convocation of the Cuban Church (Encuentro Nacional Eclesial Cubano) |
| FERES | International Federation of Socio-Religious Studies (Federación Internacional de Estudios Socio-Religiosos) |
| FEU | University Student Federation (Federación Estudiantil Universitaria) |
| ICAIC | Cuban Institute of Art and Film Industry (Instituto Cubano de Arte e Industria Cinematográfica) |
| ICAP | Cuban Institute of Friendship with Peoples (Instituto Cubano de Amistad con los Pueblos) |
| IMF | International Monetary Fund |

| | |
|---|---|
| JEC | Young Catholic Students (Juventud Estudiantil Católica) |
| JOC | Young Catholic Workers (Juventud Obrera Católica) |
| JUC | Catholic University Youth (Juventud Universitaria Católica) |
| MAP | Revolutionary People's Movement (Movimiento Revolucionario del Pueblo) |
| MRR | Movement to Recover the Revolution (Movimiento de Recuperación Revolucionaria) |
| ONIS | National Office of Social Research (Oficina Nacional de Investigación Social) |
| PCC | Cuban Communist Party (Partido Comunista de Cuba) |
| REC | Cuban Church in Reflection (Reflexión Eclesial Cubana) |
| UMAP | Military Units to Aid Production (Unidades Militares de Ayuda a la Producción) |
| UNESCO | United Nations Educational, Scientific and Cultural Organization |

Medellín Conference—Second General Conference of Latin American Bishops, Medellín, Columbia, 1968

Puebla Conference—Third General Conference of Latin American Bishops, Puebla, Mexico, 1979

Río de Janeiro Conference—First General Conference of Latin American Bishops, Río de Janeiro, Brazil, 1955

# Notes

## Foreword

1. See, for example, Manuel Fernández, *Religión y Revolución en Cuba: Veinticinco Años de Lucha Ateísta* (Miami: Saeta Ediciones, 1984), and Pablo M. Alfonso, *Cuba, Castro y los Católicos: Del Humanismo Revolucionario al Marxismo Totalitario* (Miami: Ediciones Hispamerican Books, 1985).
2. *Documento Final, Encuentro Nacional Eclesial Cubano* (Havana: mimeo, 1986), p. 7.

## Introduction

1. Long after I undertook this work but before I finished—as is evident in the work itself—the whole Cuban Catholic church plunged into the Cuban Church in Reflection (REC). At the request of the hierarchy I made some modest personal contributions. One aspect of the REC was its "re-reading" of the history of the Cuban church, with a greater degree of scholarly and self-critical rigor than ever before. Despite differences of style and language, sometimes unfortunately harsh on my part, I believe the institutional focus and my own have a great deal in common in the way they assess things, if one makes allowance for the diversity of viewpoints. It has been said that my own viewpoint of the church seems to be from the "outside." This well-meaning observation comes from a friend, a cleric, and it obviously comes from someone who, despite his own frequent sorties "outside," lives a settled life *ad intra*. My different point of view is perhaps my greatest contribution to the church of which I am an active member. A nonbeliever might say just the opposite about my viewpoint. Thus it is up to my readers to assess—or dismiss—my effort and it will be the task of true historians to straighten it out

and improve on it with the scholarly rigor that has been beyond my reach.

2. It is fitting to mention with gratitude the unselfish support, collaboration, and contributions given me, in different ways and degrees, during the preparation of this work, by Archbishops Francisco Oves and Jaime Ortega of Havana; Bishop Carlos Manuel de Céspedes; the late Dr. Julio Morales Gómez; Fathers Ramón Suárez Polcari, René David, and José Félix Pérez; the historian of our city, Eusebio Leal Spengler; Jorge Ramírez Calzadilla of the group working on religious sociology in the Academy of Sciences; the outstanding intellectual, Cintio Vitier; journalists Walfredo Piñera, Juan Emilio Friguls, and Enrique López Oliva; the educator Lourdes López; the Catholic lay leader Srta. Gina Preval, and the many others who provided help while this volume was being prepared.

## 1. The General Situation of the Church

1. Data taken from the report to CELAM's First General Conference, "Resumen de las Respuestas del Episcopado de Cuba al Cuestionario de la Sagrada Congregación Consistorial para la Conferencia de Latinoamérica en Río de Janeiro [Summary of the Responses of the Cuban Bishops to the Questionnaire of the Sacred Consistorial Congregation for the Latin American Conference in Río de Janeiro]—Havana, March 30, 1955," from the archives of the Bishops Conference of Cuba.
2. The Servite third order was headquartered in the main religious house of the Franciscan Fathers in Havana and brought together all those men and women who followed the Franciscan way of life but who could not belong to the third order of St. Francis because they were black.
3. This statistic was published by the Catholic University Association in a pamphlet published in 1956, but it was not widely known until it was picked up by *Bohemia* magazine (Havana, Mar. 22, 1968).
4. See n. 3, above.
5. Ibid.
6. Ibid.
7. Ibid.
8. In 1949 Cuba raised its diplomatic office in the Vatican to the status of an embassy. The first ambassador was Alfonso Forcade.

## 2. Uneasiness (1959–1960)

1. Special issue, "Siglo y Cuarto del Diario de la Marina," Havana, Sept. 15, 1957, p. 24.

2. See *Memoria del Congreso Católico Nacional,* published in Havana.
3. *Boletín de las Provincias Eclesiásticas de la República de Cuba* year 43 (Jan.–Feb. 1960), nos. 1–2, pp. 8ff.
4. Ibid., pp. 13ff.
5. Ibid., pp. 211ff.
6. Ibid., pp. 32ff.
7. Ibid., p. 5.
8. This suspension is one of those governed by the Catholic church's old Code of Canon Law for different infractions of ecclesiastical discipline. The one suspended is forbidden to exercise "any act of the power of orders whether acquired by ordination or by privilege" (Canon 2279, 2, no. 2).
9. *Boletín de las Provincias Eclesiásticas de la República de Cuba* year 43 (July–Aug. 1960), nos. 7–8, pp. 146ff.
10. Ibid.

## 3. Confrontation (1961–1962)

1. After the failed Bay of Pigs invasion, the church temporarily closed the diocesan seminaries. Minor seminarians were sent home and the major seminarians of El Buen Pastor in Havana were sent to finish their studies overseas. Some of them returned to Cuba after ordination, although a few left the country for good.
2. Father Chaurrondo, who began parish missions in Cuba and missionary work among prisoners, wrote a day-by-day account, starting with the March 1952 coup by Fulgencio Batista and continuing until just before he went back to Spain, where he died shortly afterward. One copy was sent to the headquarters of the Vincentian Fathers and others were kept in the chancery office and in the parish house of La Merced of the Vincentian Fathers in Havana.

## 4. Flight (1963–1967)

1. After his retirement for reasons of health, Bishop Alfredo Llaguno died, on Aug. 20, 1979, at the age of seventy-seven after fifty-one years as a priest. There was an impressive turnout for his funeral. All the Cuban bishops were there except for Archbishop Francisco Oves, who was in Rome. Bishop Fernando Azcárate offered the final words in the Colón Cemetery.

## 5. Re-encounter (1968–1978)

1. Supplement of *Vida Cristiana,* no. 327, Sunday, Apr. 27, 1969, published in Havana with ecclesiastical permission by Father Donato Cavero, a Jesuit.
2. Copy of the original version of "Resumen de Conclusiones y Sugerencias," from this meeting, is in the author's files.
3. After resigning from the archdiocese of Havana, Archbishop Evelio Díaz spent his last years in a modest apartment with his family in Havana despite offers of more comfortable places to live, from both church and state authorities. After a long illness he died on July 21, 1984. His funeral was a massive demonstration of general mourning.
4. *Granma,* May 1, 1971.
5. *CUBA-CHILE* (Havana: Ediciones Políticas, Comisión de Orientación Revolucionaria del Comité Central del Partido Comunista de Cuba, 1972), p. 268, col. 1.
6. Ibid., p. 17, col. 2.
7. Ibid., p. 418, col. 1.
8. Ibid., p. 278, col. 2.
9. Ibid., p. 441, col. 1.
10. *Primer Encuentro Latinoamericano de Cristianos por el Socialismo* (Havana: Ediciones Camilo Torres, 1973).
11. Juan J. Ramos, in Ramiro Guerra y Sánchez, et al., eds., *Historia de la Nación Cubana* (Havana, 1952), vol. 2, p. 302.
12. Father Carlos Manuel de Céspedes was one of those major seminarians who upon finishing their philosophy courses at San Carlos Seminary in 1959 were sent by their archbishop to continue their theological studies in Rome. After he returned to Cuba in 1963 he stood out for his understanding of the Cuban revolutionary process. His public statement, "I am not a Marxist but I'm not a *gusano* either" [lit. "worm," i.e., "counterrevolutionary"] upset the *gusanos* in both Cuba and Miami (see the Mexican magazine *Sucesos,* Sept. 17, 1966, p. 15). These sectors opposed to the revolution were even more upset that Father Céspedes should accept the revolutionary government's invitation to sit at the presidential tribunal, where the whole country could see him on television, seated next to Fidel Castro, in the official ceremony commemorating the 100th anniversary of the Grito de Yara [Cry of Yara], which launched the uprising of Cubans led by the founding father—and great-great-grandfather of the young priest—Carlos Manuel de Céspedes, on his farm La Demajagua, and which started the wars for Cuban independence.

13. The document of Cuban Catholics at the synod "was run off at the Havana chancery office through the kindness of His Excellency Archbishop [Oves]," as was stated at the bottom of the copies its authors sent to the bishops, clergy, and lay leaders in Cuba. It was also reprinted and criticized in the Spanish publication *Reunión* (newsletter of the Instituto de Estudios Cubanos de Madrid), nos. 69–70 (Jan.–Feb. 1975), pp. 2–3, and in other foreign publications.
14. *Plataforma Programática del Partido Comunista de Cuba, Tesis y Resoluciones* (Havana: Departamento de Orientación Revolucionaria del Comité Central del Partido Comunista de Cuba, 1976), p. 100.
15. *Plataforma Programática,* p. 101. This programmatic line is consistent with statements made by Fidel Castro on the matter from the moment of revolutionary victory. At an event held at the headquarters of the Cuban Workers Federation [CTC; Central de Trabajadores de Cuba] in 1960, Fidel said, "There is no reason we should have problems with the church. The revolutionary government is not at all concerned, nor should it be concerned. On the contrary, the revolutionary government is happy it can proclaim the right of any citizen to engage in any religious practice. There is no reason for the revolution to prohibit any priest from praying, preaching, or practicing his religion, whether he be Catholic, Protestant, Muslim, or any other religion" (Baldomero Alvarez Ríos, *Cuba: Revolución e Imperialismo* [Havana: Editorial Ciencias Sociales, Instituto del Libro, 1969], p. 222).
16. *Plataforma Programática,* p. 101.
17. Ibid., pp. 101–2.
18. *Tesis y Resoluciones. Primer Congreso del Partido Comunista de Cuba* (Havana: Departamento de Orientación Revolucionaria del Comité Central del Partido Comunista de Cuba, 1976), p. 304.
19. *Tesis y Resoluciones,* pp. 305–6.
20. Cuban believers should appreciate the sensitivity shown by the Cuban Workers Federation (CTC) at the large mass demonstration held in the Plaza de la Revolución in Havana, Dec. 22, 1975, when the members of the Central Committee of the party elected at the First Congress were presented to the public. On the songsheet with the words to the "Internationale," to be sung at the end of the ceremony, the verse that begins "No more supreme saviors, neither Caesar, nor the bourgeois nor God" was dropped. Since that time the anthem of the world proletariat has been sung in this shortened version in Cuba, at least in public ceremonies.
21. This statement by the Cuban bishops was noted in *Granma,* Nov.

16, 1976, and also in the Catholic Sunday publication *Vida Cristiana,* Nov. 9, 1976.

22. One of the two Cuban exiles jailed in Venezuela for this incident was Luis Posada. Subsequently he broke out (or bribed his way out) of jail. He was part of the contra-supply operation at Ilopango airport in El Salvador, the airport from which Eugene Hasenfus flew. Posada's associate, Felix Rodriguez (aka Max Gomez), has been linked to George Bush, through Bush's aide Donald Gregg, a connection Bush has tried to make light of. – ED.
23. On Nov. 15, 1976, *Granma* published the full texts of the messages of condolence sent by the Holy See and by Archbishop Francisco Oves of Havana, to the government, the Cuban people, and relatives of the victims of the destruction of the Cuban plane in Barbados.
24. The complete text of the dialogue between Fidel Castro and the church representatives in Jamaica was published in Cuba in *Granma,* Nov. 3, 1977, p. 2, and reprinted by the Research Center [Centro de Estudios] of the Ecumenical Council of Cuba for distribution at the Eighth National Camilo Torres Conference, held Feb. 24, 1978. For the English translation, see Appendix 3 of Sergio Arce, *The Church and Socialism* (New York: Circus, 1985).
25. The continuing political, ideological, and cultural relevance of Father Varela in the social awareness of Cuba, even during the building of socialism along the lines of the Marxist-Leninist atheistic theory, was evidenced in the fact that the revolutionary government attached the name "Félix Varela" to its highest honor. That honor was established in order "to recognize extraordinary contributions by Cuban citizens and foreigners in support of the imperishable values of our national culture and universal culture" (cf. Law no. 30, of the State Council of the Republic, headed by Fidel Castro, dated Nov. 10, 1979, art. 4, sec. 14).
26. Archbishop Oves's words at the Eleventh Festival of Youth and Students were published in the magazine *Heraldo Cristiano* (Presbyterian Reformed Church in Cuba), 24, nos. 9–10 (1978): 16ff.
27. The statement of the Catholic Bishops of Cuba on dialogue with the Cuban community living outside Cuba, along with similar statements made by Christian churches and ecumenical institutions in Cuba, was published in a special edition of the magazine *Mensaje,* put out by the Ecumenical Council of Cuba (year 6, January–March 1979, no. 20).

    Within the context of this incipient dialogue, several Cuban priests and religious who had left during the early years of the revolution were soon to visit Cuba after many years of being away. These visits were on a private basis, though some people came in groups. An especially important visit was that by twenty-one Cuban priests and religious who came from the Dominican Republic and Puerto Rico. Accompanying them was the CELAM leader Bishop Roque Adames Rodríguez, of Santiago de los Caballeros in the Dominican Republic.

28. See above, chap. 3, sec. "*La Caridad* Procession."
29. The deaths of Their Holinesses, Popes Paul VI and John Paul I, because they were both chief of state of the Vatican as well as pontiff of the universal Catholic church, and because that state maintains diplomatic relations with the Cuban state, were observed in Cuba in accordance with what the State Council decreed in both cases: "three days of official mourning with the flag at half mast over public buildings and military facilities" during those days (cf. decrees of the State Council for Aug. 7 and Sept. 29, 1978, in the *Gazeta Oficial de la República,* special issues 13 and 14, on those dates). The revolutionary Cuban government had done the same when Pope John XXIII died in 1963.
30. The importance of the Medellín Conference prompted groups of well-known lay Catholics to publish a "Reflection" on July 10, 1978, which begins with a critical analysis of the situation of the Catholic church in Cuba during the twenty years of socialist revolution. On Jan. 14, 1979, these reflection groups sent an "Exhortation" to the bishops meeting in the Puebla Conference. Archbishop Francisco Oves of Havana, president of the Bishops Conference of Cuba, took it to the Puebla Conference as an unofficial document. Both documents were independently reprinted in different parts of the world. (See CRIE [Centro Regional de Informaciones Ecuménicas, Servicio Especial del Centro de Documentación, Ocotepec 39, San Jerónimo, Mexico 20, D.F.], Jan. 1979, p. 16; and CENCOS, [Centro Nacional de Comunicación Social, Servicios Especiales de Prensa, Medellín 33, Mexico 7, D.F.], Serie Puebla 790, Indice de Informacion, Bulletins nos. 11, 12, 37, 41.)

## 6. Dialogue (1979–1985)

1. See above, chap. 5, sec. "The Eleventh World Festival of Youth and Students."
2. This pronuncio demonstrated that he did not understand the Cuban situation. One example among others was the fact that he

criticized what Archbishop Oves said on occasions such as the celebration of the Virgin in 1978 in Havana. He also impeded Archbishop Oves's relations with CELAM and at the Puebla Conference. The withdrawal of Tagliaferri from Cuba after the Puebla Conference came as a surprise.

3. *Granma,* Nov. 25, 1981, p. 3, col. 6.
4. See above, chap. 4, sec. "Obligatory Military Service."
5. *Vida Cristiana,* no. 853, Sept. 28, 1980.
6. Pronuncio Einaudi comes from the family of the Christian Democrat who was president of Italy shortly after the defeat of Italian fascism. Other members of that family are the head of the progressive Italian publishing firm, Einaudi, and Luigi Einaudi, who has been a professor of political science at universities in southwestern United States and an adviser to the White House from within the U.S. State Department. He was the main figure involved in the well-known report on the situation of the Catholic church in Latin America published by the Rand Corporation in the late 1960s.
7. *Granma,* Dec. 9, 1981, p. 3, col. 4.
8. *Granma,* July 28, 1980, p. 2, cols. 2ff.
9. See the Working Document of ENEC, p. 17.
10. See *II Congreso del Partido Comunista de Cuba: Documentos y Discursos* (Havana: Ed. Politica, 1981), pp. 412ff., esp. 413–14.
11. During the celebration of the Second Congress of the PCC, something highly significant happened. It was probably quite interesting to many of our foreign visitors, especially Latin Americans, Spaniards, French, Italians, and people from other capitalist countries, judging from how often they ask whether believers can be members of the Cuban Communist party. All the first-run movie houses in the country showed a documentary called *Cayita: Leyenda y Gesta* [Cayita: Legend and Exploits] produced by ICAIC (Instituto Cubano de Arte e Industria Cinematográfica; Cuban Institute of Art and Film Industry) and directed by the Cuban filmmaker Luis Felipe Bernaza. The documentary deals with aspects of the life of the revolutionary, elderly Cuban woman named Leocadia Araujo, who was called "Cayita" and who died a few years later. In the film Cayita herself narrates how, despite the fact that she said she was a practicing Catholic, she received a PCC membership card by a decision of the party's first secretary, Fidel Castro. With regard to opinions by well-known Cuban Christians about believers being active members of the party, one may check the interviews pub-

lished in the Basque-Spanish magazine *Herria 2000 Eliza,* no. 21 (April 1980), pp. 25ff.

12. *L'Osservatore Romano,* weekly edition in Spanish, July 10, 1983, p. 7, photo caption.
13. Ibid., p. 7, cols. 2–3; *Vida Cristiana,* no. 994, Aug. 7, 1983, back, col. 2.
14. *L'Osservatore Romano,* July 10, 1983, p. 7, col. 4; *Vida Cristiana,* nos. 994–95, Aug. 14, 1983.
15. Ibid., p. 8, cols. 3, 1; *Vida Cristiana,* no. 995.
16. Ibid., p. 8, col. 1; *Vida Cristiana,* no. 995.
17. Ibid.
18. For a general overview of the contents, see *Vida Cristiana,* nos. 1017–20, 1022–23, 1038–40, dated Jan. 15, 22, 29; Feb. 5, 19, 26; and June 10, 17, 24; see also "Mensaje de la Asamblea Arquidiocesana de la Habana a la REC" (Message of the Archdiocesan Assembly of Havana to the "Cuban Church in Reflection"), its "Lineas de Fuerza" (main lines), and the homily of Archbishop Jaime Ortega at the Mass that concluded that meeting on July 23, 1985, which were published by the Archdiocese of Havana. On the proposal for ENEC, see *Vida Cristiana,* no. 115 (Dec. 10, 1985), and subsequent issues, in addition to the pre-draft and the much improved Working Document.
19. During the 1960s the nuncio, Monsignor Zacchi, told the author that in the course of official conversation Fidel Castro said that the church should not ask him to demand that his colleagues in the revolution show greater respect for Catholics, but rather, that church people should help him by making Catholics more worthy of respect so that they could not but be respected. Moreover, in keeping with the political line on religion laid down in the two party congresses, the party's Department of Organization in May 1984 pointed out to all its cells and militants some errors committed with regard to believers. The department pointed out also that the fact that a person is a believer does not in itself mean that he or she has a negative attitude toward the revolution, and it was suggested that an effort should be made to examine each particular case. The party, further, reminded its members of the obligation to observe strictly the legal regulations about these problems. (See "Información Interna para Núcleos," May 1984, published by the Departamento de Organización del CC; pp. 5ff.)
20. See *Juventud Rebelde,* July 5, 1985, p. 1, cols. 4–5.
21. *Fidel y la Religión: Conversaciones con Frei Betto,* ed. Frei Betto

(Havana: Editorial del Consejo de Estado, 1985), p. 285. English trans.: *Fidel and Religion* (New York: Simon and Schuster, 1987).

22. See the Italian weekly magazine *Famiglia Cristiana,* no. 48 (Dec. 2, 1984), pp. 70ff., and news cables of AFP (France-Presse news agency).
23. *Fidel y la Religión,* pp. 315, 316.
24. Ibid., pp. 317–18.
25. Ibid., pp. 318–20.
26. Ibid., p. 320.
27. In this long-distance dialogue between Fidel Castro and Pope John Paul II, it was significant that the Holy See donated $20,000 to the Cuban revolutionary government to help repair the damage caused by Hurricane "Kate," which ravaged the island in November 1985 (see *Granma,* Feb. 1, 1986, last page, col. 3).
28. See *Granma, Juventud Rebelde, Trabajadores,* and *Tribuna de la Habana* for June 20, 1984. Fidel's physical presence in a church during worship and the fact that he spoke to those present was perhaps the reason the articles, photos, and television coverage were so extensive. (See also *Fidel y la Religión,* p. 255.)
29. See *Granma,* Dec. 22, 1984, pp. 1, 3; *Bohemia,* year 76, no. 52 (Havana, Dec. 19, 1984), pp. 48–49.
30. *Granma,* "Resumen Semanal," Feb. 3, 1985.
31. Ibid.
32. Ibid., p. 5, col. 5, at the end.
33. Ibid., p. 1, col. 2.
34. See *Vida Cristiana,* no. 1116 (Dec. 8, 1985), and *Fidel y la Religión,* p. 269.
35. *Granma,* Feb. 1, 1985.
36. See above, sec. "An Ecumenical Meeting with the Rev. Jesse Jackson."
37. See *Granma,* Oct. 17, 1985, and the complete text in *Vida Cristiana,* no. 1108, Oct. 13, 1985.
38. See n. 21, above.
39. *Fidel y la Religión,* p. 249 (in the English translation see pp. 214–15); also "La Voz de Nuestro Obispo: Dialogo entre creyentes y ateos," in *Vida Cristiana,* no. 1075, Feb. 24, 1985, and above, n. 2.
40. Cf. "*Fidel y la Religión*: una solución y un reto" (*Fidel and Religion*: A Solution and a Challenge), a paper given by Gómez Treto at an ecumenical meeting of Cuban Christian leaders to discuss the book, held in Havana on Jan. 13, 1986, under the sponsorship of the Research Center of the Ecumenical Council of

Cuba. The center will publish this paper along with other papers and statements made on that occasion.

41. "*Fidel y la Religión*: una solución y un reto," and also the publication *JUPRECU* put out by the Presbyterian Youth of Cuba, year 11 (1972), nos. 5–6, p. 11.

# Index